DEEP LOVE

A COLLECTION OF BIOGRAPHICAL, PROFESSIONAL AND PHILOSOPHICAL ESSAYS

DR. KHALID SOHAIL

Copyright

Published in 2019 by Green Zone Publishing
A division of Dr. Sohail MPC Inc.
213 Byron St. South
Whitby, Ontario Canada L1N 4P7
T. 905- 666-7253, F. 905-666-4397
E-mail: welcome@drsohail.com
Website: www.drsohail.com

Deep Love
Sohail, K (Khalid), 1952 –

ISBN – 978-1-927874-30-1
　　1.　Biographical　2. Professional and Philosophical Essays

Edited by:　　　　Aisha Ashraf
Cover Design:　　Shahid Shafiq

A collection of biographical, professional and philosophical essays

Special thanks to

Shahid Shafiq for designing the book cover,

Aisha Ashraf for offering creative suggestions to the content of the book

and

Marcelina Naini for formatting the book.

CONTENTS

INTRODUCTION

WHEN DREAMS COME TRUE   1

BIOGRAPHICAL ESSAYS
1.   Deep Love   10
2.   My Wise Father Basit   12
3.   In Memory Of My Poet Uncle Arif   16
4.   My Loving Sister Amber   19
5.   Family Of The Heart: My Close and
      Creative Friends   21

PROFESSIONAL ESSAYS
6.   Dr. Hoenig and A Pregnant Girl   26
7.   Dr. Wolf and A Miracle Of Healing
      Relationship   29
8.   Light at The End Of The Tunnel
      From Melancholy to Depression   33
9.   The Last Hope   38
10.   Three Hours in Court   41
11.   Developing A Community
      Mental Health Program   44
12.   Creating a Meaningful Life   48

CREATIVE ESSAYS
13.   From Creative Rain To Creative Spring   54
14.   Creative Miscarriages   59
15.   Story Telling and Story Writing   62
16.   Mystic Poetry   67
17.   Raising Social and Political Consciousness   76

PHILOSOPHICAL ESSAYS

18.   Human Psyche: Soul Or Mind?   82
19.   Science and Spirituality   86
20.   Secular Spirituality   104
21.   God Is a Metaphor   110
22.   Seven Causes of Human Suffering   114
23.   Seven Reasons To Kill   118
24.   From Tribalism To Humanism   122
25.   The Role of Mystics, Artists and Scientists
       In *Human Evolution*   126
26.   Seven Humanist Philosophers   130

REVIEWS

27.   Goodbye Islam, Hello Humanism
       by Gabrielle Bauer   138
28.   Verum, Ipsum, Factum by Munir Saami   141
29.   The Next Stage of Human Evolution
       by Farzana Hassan   145
30.   Dr. Khalid Sohail: Spiritualism As *Secular
       Humanism by Ishtiaq Ahmed*   151
31.   Faiz, A Poet Of Peace From Pakistan
       by Arif Waqar   154
32.   Love Letters to Humanity
       by Zia-ud-din   159
33.   Love Letters To Humanity
       by Shahid Akhter   163
34.   A Broken Man reviewed by Ikram Brelvi   172
35.   From Holy War To Global Peace
       by Farzana Hassan   177
36.   Dr. Sohail's Relentless Search for Peace
       by Sehdev Kumar   181
37.   The Man Fate Brought Back
       By Syed Haider   184
38.   My Journey Of Thirty Years With Sohail
       by Anne Henderson   187
39.   Two Thought Provoking Books In One
       by Syed Haider   193

40.   Words, Words and Words reviewed by
      Ishtiaq Ahmed   202
41.   Words, Words and Words and The Seeker
      by Aisha Isabel Ashraf   207
42.   In Quest Of... The Seeker
      by Christen Junker-Andersen   214
43.   Dr Khalid Sohail's *Deep Love*
      by Zahir Anwar   218

WHEN DREAMS COME TRUE
presented at the
Family Of The Heart Seminar Dec 15th, 2013

Ladies and Gentlemen,

I would like to start by thanking my dear friends for organizing this seminar and celebrating my new books. A couple of weeks ago when the invitation of the seminar was circulated I asked myself, "What would I like to share with you people in this seminar?" The first thought that came to my mind was that the city of Toronto has played a significant role in my creative journey. My creativity was the seed, and literary atmosphere of Toronto was the fertile soil in which the creative seed turned into a plant and grew to be a tree and produced literary fruits in the form of poems and stories and essays and interviews and books and documentaries in Urdu as well as English. It is still a mystery for me how I started as an Urdu writer in Pakistan and transformed into an English writer in Canada. So I want to publicly acknowledge the role Toronto, my creative and humanist friends of the Family of the Heart, and my creative colleagues of Creative Psychotherapy Clinic, that include Anne Henderson and Bette Davis, played in my literary, creative and philosophical growth.

When I reflect on my past as a writer, humanist and psychotherapist, I realize that quite early in life I fell in love with literature, art and philosophy and I realized that they could be useful in discovering my truth, inspiring others and serving humanity. When I reflect on my life- long love to serve humanity I remember two couplets, one of Faiz Ahmed Faiz and the other one of Arif Abdul Mateen.

The first couplet is

Faiz thi raah sar basar manzil
Hum jahan pohunchay kamiyaab aaye
[Faiz, every step on the way was a destination
we were successful wherever we were]
And the second couplet is

Bas aik saboot apni wafa ka hay mairay paas
Main apni nigahoN main gunahgaar nahiN hooN
[I have only one proof of my love and faithfulness
I am not guilty in my own eyes]

At an early age I also realized that all creative people, whether poets or philosophers, artists or mystics, painters or playwrights, scientists or scholars, reformers or revolutionaries, psychologists or psychotherapists, have a creative personality and a creative philosophy that guides them in their creative expression and creative communication. They have profound and deep love in their hearts for humanity. Khalil Gibran once wrote, "Don't you ever think you can guide love. If love finds you worthy she will guide you." I feel fortunate that love for humanity has been guiding me. It helped me overcome my fear that I expressed in my short poem titled

APPREHENSION

I am afraid
The noise of the outside world
Will drown one day
The music inside.

I realized that love was closely connected with creativity and creativity was intimately connected with freedom. I became aware that there were two kinds of freedom, inner freedom that dealt with freedom of thought and imagination and outer freedom that dealt with freedom of expression and action that was intimately connected with the limitations, restrictions and inhibitions imposed on the creative personalities by their conservative families, communities and cultures. Success of the creative personalities depended on how they kept their inner music alive and how they coped with outer limitations. One of my couplet reflects my views about freedom
Apni parwaz ka andaza laganay kay liay
Apnay mahaul say aazaad fizaiN maNgheeN
[I asked for open spaces
To know how high I can fly]

Let me share with you a few highlights of my creative journey from the age 16 to 61. When I was a teenager I became aware that my life was a special gift that nature had given to me. I asked myself, 'How can I make my life meaningful and successful? What would be the best use of this special gift?" So I came up with four dreams about my life.

My first dream was to become a doctor and a specialist. I thought I would serve humanity better as a psychiatrist than a family physician, as I would be able to help my patients and their families, in their emotional suffering that can be more painful than physical suffering. I think watching my father have a nervous breakdown as a child and my mom looking after him must have unconsciously influenced me to become a psychiatrist. I wanted to study until the age of 30 and then serve my patients for another 30 years and then retire. At the age of 16 I could not imagine living more than 60. This is an interesting coincidence that I received my FRCP in psychiatry 3 weeks before my 30th birthday in 1982. After getting my Fellowship I served as a psychotherapist in different hospitals and clinics for 30 years. So now at the age of 61, I can say that I successfully fulfilled my first dream.

My second dream was to become a writer and write a series of books. As a teenager I was impressed by writers like Saadat Hasan Minto and Ismat Chughtai, Sigmund Freud and Carl Jung, Viladmir Lenin and Mao ze Tung. All of them had created a body of work. They were like marathon runners and I wanted to develop the attitude of a marathon runner rather than a 100 meter sprinter. So, for the last forty years, I have been consistently writing and I have been successful in creating nearly 40 books. So my second dream also came true.

My third dream was to travel the world. Rather than reading the books of History and Geography I wanted to visit different parts of the world and meet people of different cultures and see how they lived. So after receiving my Canadian Passport in 1982 I went to Israel and South Africa, two countries to which I could not travel on a Pakistani Passport. After that I traveled in North America and South Africa, Latin America and the Middle East and visited Russia and the Scandinavian Countries. Of all the countries I traveled, three cities that inspired me the most were Jerusalem, Paris and Athens as they were full of history and art and mythology. After the 9/11 tragedy, traveling was not as enjoyable as before but I felt that I had already fulfilled my third dream.

The fourth dream was to create a circle of creative friends. After meeting Ashfaq, moving to Toronto, and getting involved in the publication of *Urdu International*, I met many creative friends like Jawaid Danish in USA, Abrar Hasan in France, Saeed Anjum in Norway, Nasar Malik in Denmark, Sain Sucha in Sweden, Yousaf Hasan in Pakistan and Zahir Anwar in India. I interviewed many scholars who visited Canada from India and Pakistan including Kishawar Naheed and Fehmida Riaz, Sharib Rudoulvi and Gopi Chand Narang, Abdullah Hussain and Saqi Farooqi and many more.

After I published my book *From Islam to Secular Humanism,* I met many humanist friends from different religious and cultural backgrounds and presented papers in many Humanist seminars and conferences. So I fulfilled my fourth dream also.

While I was fulfilling my dreams I realized that I, like many other creative personalities, had to face different challenges and overcome different obstacles before I could be successful. I can share four challenges that I can identify. In Urdu they can be named as *rawayat, hijrat, dualat and shohrat.* [Tradition, immigration, wealth and fame]

My first challenge was tradition. My family wanted me to have a traditional marriage and live a traditional family life. I realized quite early that if I wanted to be a successful writer and therapist, I had to choose a non-traditional lifestyle. So I did not choose a traditional family life. For me family life was a fulltime job and being a writer and a therapist was also a full time job and I could not do two full time jobs in my life time. I know many creative people who tried to keep a balance between two full time jobs and finally left both of them unfinished and incomplete.

My second challenge was immigration. Very early in my life I had realized that my creative personality and non-traditional philosophy was incompatible with the traditional, conservative and religious environment of Peshawar, Pakistan. When I, shared my non-traditional views with my poet uncle Arif Abdul Mateen, he suggested that I keep quiet about my rebellious views, leave the country after my graduation and move to a Western country where I could practice what I believed. So I went to Iran and then came to Canada to study and to live. If I had stayed in Pakistan, it is quite possible that I would have been assassinated or sent to jail or landed in a mental asylum. Immigration was the second challenge I had to face.

My dear friend Rasheed Nadeem has a couplet
Ye shehyr agar zarf kushada nahiN rakhta
main bhi yahaN rehnay ke irada nahiN rakhta
[If my city is not broad minded and does not have a big heart, then I have no intentions to stay here]

My third challenge was wealth. There are so many doctors and lawyers, engineers and businessmen who are obsessed with money. In my life I have had to sacrifice materialistic gains for the sake of my ideals of serving suffering humanity and my community. I chose to become a psychotherapist and have my own clinic and treat my patients to the best of my ability rather than becoming rich. Serving humanity was dearer to me than becoming a millionaire. That was the third challenge I had to face for my ideals.

My fourth challenge was fame. I have met many writers and artists who chose fame over art. For them public relationships and appearing in newspapers and radio and TV interviews became more important than their creativity and literature, philosophy and art. I always focused on my new book and new project. I know many contemporary writers who have reached their creative menopause and have stopped writing and creating. I feel lucky that even at the age of 61, I feel young, enthusiastic and creative. I am always planning my next story and my next essay, and focusing on my next book. And in that process of planning my new creations my creative friends have always been a great inspiration.

In the end let me share with you a folktale that deals with freedom needed for creative personalities to survive and thrive. I heard that folktale as a child and it has remained a source of inspiration all of my life. The folktale is about a wolf and a dog. The wolf used to live in a jungle and enjoyed his freedom. When he was young, he was healthy and happy, excited and energetic and he had no problem running fast and catching his prey. But when he got older and weaker he became afraid that he might not be able to catch his prey and starve and die a desperate and miserable death. One day while he was walking on the outskirts of the jungle, he met a healthy, handsome and well-nourished dog. He asked the dog the secret of his happiness. The dog said that he had a master who fed him and kept him in his house. The wolf asked the dog if he would introduce him to his master and the wolf could spend his old age with them. The dog had no problem and asked him to come to the same place the next day to meet his master. When the wolf heard that promise he became happy and hopeful about his future for a few seconds. But when the dog turned, the wolf saw some hair missing on his neck. On asking the dog shared that his master had a bad temper and used to tie him down with a chain in the basement for a few days when he was angry. Missing hair was the reminder of the chain. Seeing the missing hair and hearing dog's story about his master, the wolf reflected for a few seconds and then withdrew his request.

That folktale of the free wolf and the chained dog has guided me on many occasions when I faced personal, professional and existential dilemmas in my life. I always identified with the struggling but free wolf rather than the well-nourished enslaved dog. I believe our freedom inspires us to face challenges and offer sacrifices for our ideals and make our lives meaningful. I feel fortunate that I could embrace my freedom and I was able to love and create and serve. Of all the stories of my life let me share one story that deals with my creativity and my move to Toronto.

In the fall of 1983, when I lived in Saint John, New Brunswick my friend Mansoor Hussain introduced me to *Urdu International* and Ashfaq Hussain and suggested that I send him my poems and stories. When I sent my first poem and short story Ashfaq invited me to meet him in Toronto and when I met him after a psychiatric conference, he suggested that I move to Toronto. So I applied in Whitby Psychiatric hospital and when I got a job as a psychiatrist I went to talk to my Psychiatrist in Chief in my hospital. Dr John Theriault told me that if I leave in Jan 1984 I have to pay 5000 dollars for breaking the contract. At that moment I thought of the wolf and the dog. So I took out my cheque book and wrote a cheque for 5000 dollars and gave him with my resignation. Dr Theriault was shocked and had a heart attack and died after 48 hours and I moved to Toronto. My story of moving to Toronto started with my introduction with Mansoor Hussain and Ashfaq Hussain and has evolved to my introduction with Ameer Hussain. I feel very fortunate to have such wonderful friends. They are all members of my Family of the Heart. They remain my sources of ongoing inspiration.

In the end I would like to acknowledge Nelson Mandela who left us this week. He is a source of inspiration for many. Let me read you one his love letters to humanity. He said, "No one is born hating another person because of the colour of his skin, or his background or his religion. People learn to hate, and if they can learn to hate, they can be taught to love, for love comes more naturally to the human heart than its opposite. "

PART ONE

Biographical Essays

1.   DEEP LOVE

One of my childhood memories is watching my dad, Basit writing long letters to my uncle Arif. My dad had become a mystic, a deeply religious person, and people used to call him *Sufi Sahib,* while my uncle was a socialist writer and an atheist. My uncle never responded to my dad's letters and I remember one day teasing him saying, "Dad, Uncle Arif never responds because he never reads them." He smiled and said, "Son, they are love letters, not business letters."

After ten years of receiving those long, long letters, when my uncle published his new collection of poems he dedicated it to my dad. The dedication told me that he not only read those letters, but he read them very carefully and was inspired by them. Later on, my uncle also became a mystic poet.

Over the years I have reflected on my dad's long letters. I think most brothers, not getting any response, would have stopped writing those letters, but my dad did not. I wondered:

What motivated him to keep writing?

Why did he not get discouraged?

Why did he not stop?

My answer to my own prolonged reflections and introspections is *Deep Love.*

My dad loved my uncle at a deep level, deeper than most brothers I know love their brothers. Those were emotional as well as philosophical letters. My dad shared his knowledge, experience and wisdom. He shared his spiritual insights. That is why once my uncle said to me, "Your dad is younger in age but older in wisdom. He is a man of integrity."

As a student of human psychology, I ask myself, "How did my dad develop that capacity for deep love?"

I think his emotional crisis had something to do with it, a crisis that family members thought was a nervous breakdown but that he considered a spiritual breakthrough. After that crisis, when he recovered and became a mystic, his capacity to love became more intense, more profound. He developed a capacity for deep love. I was fortunate to receive that deep love from him too.

Reflecting on my dad's breakdown, breakthrough and deep love, I am reminded of a time when our neighbours were digging a well in the courtyard. As a child I was fascinated.

There was no running water in our neighbourhood. People drew water from a nearby river, so the digging of a well was of great significance. After digging a few feet down we saw the water. I was thrilled. I thought the project was complete. But my dad told me that they had to dig more because the water was good to wash clothes but not suitable for drinking as it was full of impurities. After digging another twenty feet the water was clean and good enough to drink.

I sometimes wonder whether people's hearts also have two kinds of love: superficial love and deep love. Most people can only experience and share superficial love. There are only a few, like my dad, who are able to experience and share deep love and sometimes, to reach that deeper love, they have to experience a breakdown and a breakthrough. Some reach that deep love on their own through life experiences, some need a teacher and some need a therapist. I have seen many men and women in my clinical practice who were able to access deep love in their hearts after they recovered from their personal, marital, family, social and existential crises. I feel honoured that those people shared their honest feelings and struggles with me, enabling me to become a co-traveler in their therapeutic journeys. Such change is only possible when therapy is dynamic and addresses in-depth issues of personality transformation and growth. Over the years I have become a dynamic therapist and love working with those motivated people who, despite serious emotional and personality problems, are willing to take the next step in their personal growth and social maturity to get in touch with their deeper selves and experience and share deep love. I have learnt so much from them.

On reflection, I realize that receiving deep love from my dad and sharing it with my patients has helped me become a better person and serve my community and humanity at large as a humanist psychotherapist.

August 2012

2. *MY WISE FATHER BASIT*

Some years ago, in Pakistan, my dad died. One morning, during the holy month of Ramadan, while he was fasting he suffered a stroke. He was rushed to the hospital and within a few hours he left this world. I was pleased for him, that he did not suffer long because of the stroke. After a few weeks, I flew to Pakistan and attended a ceremony held in his honour and met some of his friends, neighbours and colleagues. I was touched by their respect and reverence for my dad. Meeting them made me feel proud to be his son and fortunate that I had a wise father. On my return to Canada, I wrote the following article:

IN MEMORY OF MY DAD

My dad used to say, "When kings die, their children inherit their palaces, farms, horses, boats and many other worldly belongings but when saints die, their children inherit their wisdom, their knowledge and their stories, the stories that are passed on from one generation to another and act as candles in the dark alleys of their children's and grandchildren's lives."

Thinking about my dad, I remember a number of stories, each one of them reflecting his personality and philosophy of life. I remember:

When I passed my Grade 8 examination with distinction and came first in my school, my dad's friends came to congratulate him on his son's success. He gracefully said, "He is God's gift. I am just a caretaker. I am trying my best. I am very proud that he did so well."

It took me a long time to appreciate the wisdom of his words and to realize that he not only loved me but was proud of me and respectful of my independent personality.

When I was in Grade 10, I wanted to participate in the school presidential election. Considering my popularity, my friends were confident that I would win. When I asked my dad to sign the permission papers, he refused. I was shocked.

'What's the problem, Dad?"

"Do you want to become the president?"

"Yes, I do." I was honest.

"Then you should be disqualified."

"Why is that?" I asked, bewildered.

"Because you want power and anyone who wants power is vulnerable to abuse it. Power usually corrupts people and make them arrogant."

"I do not follow your reasoning." I was persistent.

"I believe that in any community, people should choose their leader, the person they feel would serve them best, and that person should turn the offer down because of his humility. That is the spirit of democracy. People need to learn to serve not to rule. That is the fundamental difference between autocratic and democratic organizations and institutions. When we study the history of Muslims, we find some wonderful examples. When Umar bin Abdul Aziz was asked to be the Caliph and Imam abu Hanifa was requested to be the Chief Justice, they both turned the offers down. They both stated that serving the public in that capacity was too much responsibility. But when people insisted, they reluctantly accepted the position."

My dad did not sign the papers and I did not participate in the elections. But I did not follow his logic. I thought him too idealistic. Then I visited a kibbutz in Israel and appreciated his wisdom. In the kibbutz, the leaders were chosen as my dad had suggested. People insisted that the deserving genuine and sincere people took the leadership role, while the leaders were reluctant to take responsibility. That day I realized my dad's ideas were not just a fantasy. They could be acted upon provided the community was ready to adopt such a philosophy and lifestyle.

When I passed my grade twelve examination, I was excited to be among the top twenty students in the province. When the medical college turned down my application, I was brokenhearted. The college stated that I could not be accepted, as I did not have a domicile certificate of the province because my parents were immigrants from India and did not own property. After I recovered from that disappointment, I decided to apply for the Pakistan Army. It was 1969 and after the 1965 war with India, the Pakistan army was very popular. Officers were heroes in the eyes of the public. When I filled out the application form I discovered the papers had to be signed by my father. He refused. We had a heart to heart talk.

"Son, I do not want you to join the army."

"Why not?" I was curious.

"Because as a soldier you take an oath that if your commander orders "shoot" then you have to shoot."

"But everyone takes that oath."

"What if the Pakistani army starts a war with Iran or Afghanistan, our Muslim neighbours, and your commander orders, 'Shoot!' Would you kill your Muslim brothers and sisters? No, I cannot sign these papers."

My dad did not sign the papers and I did not join the army.

When I was at university, I used to come home late at night. My dad would be sleeping while my mom was always awake worrying about me. One night she kept him awake to 'talk' to me. She wanted him to scold and discipline me. That night I was nervous but I knew he was a gentle soul. He was never harsh. He had a philosophical perspective about everything he did. He took me to his room, sat in front of me and said in a gentle tone, "Son, do you know who the people are who stay up late at night?'

"No, Dad."

"They are either saints or sinners." And then he went to bed.

My dad had a good sense of humour. He used to encourage me and my younger sister, Amber, to tell jokes and stories at dinnertime. He considered that a gift for our mother.

When I started writing poetry and reciting it at university functions he shared a folktale with me. He said,

"In a village, a middle aged father of three sons was sitting on the curb crying. People asked him,

"Why are you crying?"

He said, "I have no sons left."

"What happened to the oldest one?"

"He got married."

"What about the middle son?"

"He left the village and settled in the city."

"But your youngest son has neither married nor moved to the city. What happened to him?"

"He became a poet," he said, and started crying again."

After telling the story my dad laughed and said, "I have only one son and he became a poet." I laughed too.

A few years ago when my dear friend Jawaid Danish met

my Dad at my sister's house in Lahore, he took Danish aside and said, "Now that I see how passionately Sohail is involved in literature, I understand why he never had a family. I think he is married to literature and philosophy. I understand, but I do not think his mother does."

When I visited Lahore last week, I was pleasantly surprised to meet a large circle of people who admired and adored him. They all agreed he was a man of integrity and a practicing Humanist.

In spite of our philosophical differences we were always loving to each other. He did not agree but respected my secular philosophy. I wish there were more dads like him in this world. He was not only a saint, he was also a good storyteller.

....

In the last few years since his death, I have occasionally met him in dreams where he shared his wisdom and warned me about things I was facing in my life. His memories are still a source of inspiration for me. During 2001 when America attacked Afghanistan and asked Pakistan to support the war, I was glad he had not signed my papers to join the army so that I could be on the side of peace rather than war. I had never realized my Dad had such wisdom and foresight. His philosophy inspired me to write an article "Killing In The name Of God" that was published in the Canadian Humanist magazine in the fall of 2002.

June 2003

3.   *IN MEMORY OF MY POET UNCLE ARIF*

I was introduced to my Uncle Arif through his poetry and I was introduced to poetry by Uncle Arif. When I was old enough to read, I found Uncle Arif's books in my dad's small library and felt very proud that my uncle was a famous poet. The more I read his poetry and got to know his personality and philosophy, the more my sense of pride increased. He was a caring and compassionate man full of love, peace and wisdom.

Uncle Arif lived in Lahore, while I lived in Peshawar with my parents, Basit and Aisha, and my younger sister, Amber. Whenever I went to Lahore to see my grandma, I also visited Uncle Arif to enjoy intellectually stimulating dialogue. When I asked him questions about life, he listened patiently and answered them respectfully. Many times, my younger cousin, Rozi sat close to us and listened to our dialogue. One day, as I was leaving he said to me,

"Sohail *bhai* [brother] you get more out of our dad in two hours than we get in two years."

I smiled and gave him an affectionate hug. In one of those dialogues, when I asked my uncle why people commit suicide, he shared Schopenhauer's quotation, "When the horrors of life outweigh the horrors of death, people commit suicide." My uncle had a unique clarity and distinct eloquence in articulating his thoughts.

When I was twenty, he came to visit us in Peshawar with his wife, Aunty Shehnaz. By that time, he knew that I was writing poems and short stories. My dad used to say that I was more like my uncle than him. He never felt jealous. He always encouraged my creative relationship with my uncle that he loved and respected as an older brother. A few days before he returned home, Uncle Arif took me to Green's Hotel and ordered tea and snacks and we had a heart to heart talk. I confessed that I had read dozens of books on human psychology and philosophy and studied many translations of the Quran. I no longer believed in God, scriptures, prophets and life after death. He listened to my philosophical confession, smiled and said, "My uncle, your grandpa, became an atheist at the age of 60, I became an atheist at the age of 40 and now you are becoming an atheist at the age of 20. The majority of people follow the highway of tradition, while a minority follow the trails of their hearts. Many of them are poets and philosophers, reformers and revolutionaries. You are one of them." My uncle's words were reassuring and inspiring.

In one of my visits to Lahore, I shared my poems with him. He read them carefully and marked those he considered of high literary value. My uncle's feedback helped in my selection for my first collection of poems titled *Talaash* [Searching].

After coming to Toronto, where I published five books in five years, my writer friends became quite nervous and shared their concern with me. They thought that if I wrote and published that frequently, I would become barren and stop writing. I did not believe them but I was nervous, so I consulted my uncle. After listening to my dilemma, he smiled gracefully and said, "Do not worry. Only those whose writings are primarily based on their imagination worry. In your case, they are based on your observations, experiences and encounters with life." Later on, I read the same argument by Leonard Woolf for his wife, Virginia Woolf.

By the time Uncle Arif moved to New York to live with his son Rozi, he had become old and fragile. He suffered from Parkinson's disease and depression, which is one of the complications of Parkinsonism.

When I went to New York to visit him, he told me that his time to leave this world was coming closer, he 'could hear the footsteps of death'. I thought it quite a poetic expression. Later on, he shared that he had difficulty going to the washroom at night and was afraid he might lose control of his bladder. He wanted to leave this world before he lost his self-respect.

One evening, while we were chatting he asked his granddaughter, Rabeea to get his latest poem from his bedroom so he could read it to me. While he was reciting his poem I saw a note 'incomplete' at the end of the poem. When I asked him why he wrote that, he said that the poem was unfinished and if he died suddenly in his sleep, he did not want people to think that it was a complete poem. I was impressed by this dedication to his poetry that remained till his last days. His body was failing but his mind remained active and creative till his death. He died within a few weeks of that visit.

I was touched when he published his last collection of one-line poems with this inscription, "Dedicated to my nephew Khalid Sohail, who is so much like me in his personality and

philosophy that I feel Nature has given me a new life in him."
After reading that dedication, writers all over the world found out
he was my uncle.

When he came to visit me in Toronto, I received
numerous calls from writers who wanted to talk to me. I had not
known he was so popular in Toronto. In one of the poetry
functions where he presided, he was approached by an elderly
writer, Aqeela Shaheen who asked him if he was the same Arif
who had death threats against him just after partition. Uncle Arif
said yes, he was the same Arif. On the way back, I asked him
about that incident. He explained that, when he saw thousands
of innocent men and women and children killed in partition, he
wrote a poem challenging the political leaders of Congress as
well as the Muslim League. Challenging the Muslim League and
the Pakistani government was perceived as non-patriotic and
anti-Islamic by mullahs. One evening as he traveled home, he
was surrounded by young men who told him they were going to
kill him because he had written an anti-patriotic and anti-
religious poem. When Uncle Arif showed them the poem they
apologized, realizing it was not against Islam or Pakistan, it was
against the Muslim League and the Pakistani Government. I was
impressed that my Uncle Arif had held fast to his ideas and
ideals in the face of threats and opposition. I felt proud of him.
Though he is no longer with me, I cherish his memory and his
poetry. His personality and philosophy have been a source of
inspiration long after his death. I feel proud that his collection of
poems is part of Master's course in Punjabi literature in
Pakistan. I wish there were more uncles like him in this world.

4.   *MY LOVING SISTER AMBER*

Of all my relationships with women, the most loving and wonderful is the one I have with my younger sister, Amber. She was born exactly five years after me so only one day separates our birthdays. It is quite amusing that when I celebrate my birthday on the ninth of July in Canada and call her in the evening, because of the time difference of ten hours, I find her celebrating her birthday in Pakistan. Although we have different philosophies and lifestyles we have mutual respect and admiration for each other. I feel lucky that I not only have a loving relationship with her but also a wonderful relationship with her husband Irshad Mir and their children, Afifa, Zeeshan, Arooj and Warda. I am very fond of my nephew and nieces and they are very affectionate towards me. We have an open and honest dialogue through emails. They discuss those subjects with me that they cannot discuss with their parents. They remind me of my inspiring relationship with my Uncle Arif.

A few years ago I wrote the following poems for my sister and nephew and nieces expressing my adoration and love for them.

A MIRACLE
Amber, my dear sister,
You are a living miracle.
Whenever I see you I wonder:
How could you
Inherit our parent's conflicts;
Marry a stranger;
Meet the challenges of life;
Look after the children;
Tolerate the oppressions of our time;
And still
Not give up or go insane?
It's inspiring to see you
Growing and progressing in life.
My dear sister
Come closer
Let me embrace you

You may be younger in age
But far ahead of me in life.

Sohail
December 1988

....

CHILDREN

When my nephew and nieces play with me
I become ecstatic.
When they talk to me,
My mind
Is filled with innocent perfumes.
When they tickle me,
Sparkles glow in my heart.
When they embrace me,
I feel honey tickling
In the depths of my soul.
Their mother
Looks directly into my eyes
And asks:
How long will you
Keep producing lifeless books?
When will you
Create some live babies?
I listen to her,
I smile
And remain silent.

Sohail
December 1988

5.   FAMILY OF THE HEART
MY CLOSE AND CREATIVE FRIENDS

I feel fortunate that in every phase of my life and every city I have lived in, I was able to create and maintain a wide circle of acquaintances and a small circle of very close friends. These friends became like my family and I call them my *family of the heart*. I visit them frequently and share my joys and sorrows with them. Their presence in my life doubles the excitement of my joys and divides the grief of my sorrows in half. They support me when I need them and rely on me when they are in a crisis. As I moved from one city to another, making new friends I kept in touch with the old ones through emails and phone calls and infrequent visits. That is why now I have a large circle of close friends. They are my life long earnings and I jokingly call them my emotional RRSPs.

I find it sad that I have met so many men and women, in both a personal and professional capacity, who feel lonely and unable to create close friendships. They have a small circle of acquaintances, but whenever they try to take their relationships to a higher and deeper level the relationships end mysteriously and they experience social miscarriages. Unable to have a heart-to-heart talk with their acquaintances, they do not understand the reasons for the ending of those relationships. They keep wondering what went wrong and each such social miscarriage makes them doubt themselves and their ability to maintain close bonds with others. Some of them finally give up and stop trying, considering it an exercise in futility.

When I reflect on human relationships, I feel that people meet each other, or are introduced to each other, because of a common interest—whether social or economic, religious or political, educational or cultural—and a relationship begins. The initial phase is exciting. My dear friend, Bette Davis calls it 'the phase of similarities', where two people talk about all their shared interests, hobbies, passions and dreams. But that is a honeymoon period, after which follows the 'the phase of dissimilarities' where both parties discover their differences in philosophies, personalities and lifestyles. In some cases those differences become a curse as they transform into conflicts that create tension in the relationship. In other cases those differences are a blessing and both parties learn from each other.

Every relationship faces a crisis sooner or later, and its future depends on how both parties deal with that crisis. Finding healthy ways to resolve conflicts is a key factor in creating and maintaining emotionally intimate friendships. If both parties cannot resolve the conflicts peacefully there is a cold war and both parties suffer. In my opinion if both parties cannot resolve the conflicts they can choose to gracefully and peacefully dissolve the relationship.

When I reflect on my close friendships, I realize that quite early in our relationship I identify the differences in our philosophies, personalities and lifestyles and deal with them respectfully. Let me give a few examples to highlight my point, starting with the differences in the philosophies of my friends.
My first friend is a devout Muslim.
My second friend is a determined atheist.
My third friend is a dedicated Christian.
My fourth friend is a committed Communist.
My fifth friend is a carefree agnostic.
My sixth friend is a non-committed anarchist.
Over the years, I've had lengthy dialogues with my friends—those heart-to-heart conversations I call my *homework* of friendship—to come to an agreement that respects one another's philosophy in which we do not attempt to convert each other. That homework paid well and we became comfortable with and accepted each other even when we disagreed. In many cases the friendship evolved to the point where we now enjoy the fruits of our hard work, having reached a stage where once painful intellectually stimulating discussions have become enjoyable. Since my friends read new books and authors I gain a lot of knowledge from them and I hope they learn something from me.

Alongside differences in philosophies there are also differences in lifestyles.
The first friend eats *halal* food.
The second friend requires kosher.
The third friend is a vegetarian.
The fourth one is a vegan.
I tell my friends that I avoid 3 Cs: chocolate, coffee and cheese, not for religious reasons but because I dislike the taste, the way

I dislike the taste of broccoli and diet coke. So we respect each other's wishes and go to restaurants where all of us can eat something we enjoy.

One issue capable of causing resentment in every friendship is money. Let me share something I learnt from female friends from the East as well as the West. They wanted a 50/50 arrangement so I agreed. The interesting part is that each female friend's interpretation of a fair and just 50/50 is different.

The first friend wants to have separate bills as she thinks I eat expensive steaks while she eats inexpensive vegetable dishes.

The second friend splits the bill into half, even splits the tip in the middle.

The third friend alternates. I pay one time, she pays the next time.

The fourth friend wants me to pay when we go out and when it is her turn she wants to cook a homemade meal.

The fifth friend is a socialist. She believes, as I earn 3 times more than she does, that her one dollar is equal to my three dollars. I smile and pay more than her. When my female friends ask my opinion I tell them that for me my friendship with them and spending time with them is more important than money matters.

One of the conflicts I had to deal with in my close friendships was that sometimes, when I came closer to one friend, another friend felt jealous. I tried to reassure them to resolve the conflict. In most cases this worked. In some cases I had to see those friends separately and did not bring them together as they felt uncomfortable with each other.

It has been my experience, that when people find out I do not have ulterior motives they find it easier to trust me. I like to introduce my friends to each other and become a creative bridge. My creative friends know that I try to nurture their creativity, help them finish their creative products, publish their books and then support their launch. Such support helps them enjoy their creative potential and celebrate their creative products. After creating the *Family of the Heart* organization in 2002 [which has grown from seven members to 7,000 in ten years], it has become easier for me to support and promote my creative friends and organize regular programs for them. It gives me great joy to be part of their celebrations. My creative friends also inspire me to write more and discuss my creations with them. They give me honest and sincere feedback that keeps my creative juices flowing. I believe we all need to nurture our creativity, share it with our dear ones and then find ways to serve our community and humanity.

I feel fortunate to have such true and sincere friends and I am quite willing to do my homework with them. They accept and cherish me with my idiosyncrasies, and I accept and cherish them with their eccentricities. It might be hard sometimes to resolve our personal, philosophical, creative and political conflicts but in the end it is all worth it. I always believed that growing together is better than growing in isolation. Native Indian Chief Black Elk once said 'No great work can be done by one person alone".

It is my observation that traditional people are in the majority in every community and creative people are in the minority and many times that creative minority is judged by the traditional majority. For the last decade I have been trying to support creative people in my professional life through my *Creative Psychotherapy Clinic,* and my creative friends in my social life through the *Family of the Heart.* Such an experience has been enjoyable and rewarding and I feel very proud of my circle of close and creative friends.

PART TWO

Professional Essays

6.   DR HOENIG AND A PREGNANT GIRL

The first time I met Dr John Hoenig, Professor and Chairman of the Psychiatry Department at Memorial University, Newfoundland, it was a bright October morning. I approached the switchboard operator in the General Hospital in St. Johns.

"My name is Dr Sohail and I'm here to meet Dr Hoenig. Can you help me?'

Smiling warmly, she said,

"On the front wall you can see a list of doctors. When doctors come in they press a button to announce they've arrived. Wait here and see which doctor presses the button with Dr Hoenig's name."

I thanked her and sat down to wait. After a few minutes a tall, heavyset man holding a leather briefcase and wearing a jacket and necktie entered the hospital and pressed the button. I approached him,

"Good Morning Dr Hoenig. I am Dr Sohail, the new resident."

He smiled and asked me to follow him to his office. Once there, he set down his briefcase, turned to me and explained, "Dr Sohail, today is October 9th, 1977. Your residency program will last four years and you fill finish on October 9th, 1981. After that you will get your Fellowship in Psychiatry and become one of my colleagues. Now... I want to see my first patient and you are more than welcome to join me."

Thrilled, I accompanied him as he interviewed Joanne, a 16 year old girl who was pregnant and requesting an abortion. After speaking to Joanne, Dr Hoenig asked her to wait in the waiting room and invited her mom, Grace in. Grace told us that, as a Catholic, she did not approve of abortion and if Joanne did not want to keep the baby, Grace was willing to adopt and raise her grandchild as her own child. After Grace left, I asked Dr Hoenig why he had interviewed Grace.

He explained, "Joanne can have an abortion but she is only sixteen. To do an abortion we need to give her anesthesia, and to receive anesthesia she has to sign papers giving her consent. Since she is only 16 we need to ask her mom to sign those papers and her mom, being a Catholic, is refusing.

After a few minutes Dr Hoenig asked my opinion. I told him that if the mother is refusing he should ask her dad—he would sign papers.

"What makes you so sure?" he asked.

"In my opinion," I said, "men are generally more pragmatic and less religious."

He called her dad and was pleasantly surprised when he agreed to sign the papers.

Dr Hoenig explained that in Newfoundland, for any pregnant woman to have a therapeutic abortion she has to appear before a board and get the assent of three people: her family physician, a gynaecologist and a psychiatrist.

Next Thursday morning, when Joanne came to have her abortion, I was shocked to see a long line of nuns and priests outside the hospital holding banners stating,

" *Abortion is Murder.*"

"*We want adoption not abortion.*"

Interviewing Joanne and Grace reminded me of Farheen Gul, a married woman I had seen as a patient in Pakistan when I was doing my internship in Obstetrics in the Women's Hospital. She wanted to have an abortion because she had six children and did not want a seventh child. She could not afford to feed those children. When I approached my professor she told me that abortion was illegal in Pakistan and we could not offer her that service. I felt guilty turning down her request but I was helpless. Despite my sympathy, I could do nothing without the support of my professor.

I saw that patient again after two weeks. She arrived in the operating room from Emergency on a stretcher. She was unconscious. Her sister explained she had gone to see a quack in the dark alleys of downtown Peshawar where a midwife had tried to induce an illegal abortion and ruptured her uterus in the process. My professor agreed to admit her as her life was in danger. Once more, guilt reminded me that, had we helped her two weeks earlier, she need not have gone through that pain and suffering. Fortunately, she was operated upon and her life was saved.

Over the years, I came to realize there are women all over the world, whether in Pakistan or Canada, who did not have reproductive rights. Men, whether fathers or husbands, gynaecologists or psychiatrists, have been making choices for them. I was so glad to learn that, in Canada Dr Henry Morgentaler fought for the rights of women. He was taken to court but stood firm and made sacrifices for his ideals. We now have Morgentaler clinics all over the country where women can receive an abortion if they choose. We do not want children who are not welcomed into this world by loving parents and families.

I hope for such clinics in all communities, countries and cultures all over the world, so that women can have reproductive rights and determine their own lives.

April 2012

7. DR. WOLF AND THE MIRACLE OF A HEALING RELATIONSHIP

"Your emotional life is not written in cement during childhood.
You write each chapter as you go along."

Harry Stack Sullivan

When I started my Psychiatric Residency at the Memorial University of Newfoundland in October 1977, I had the intellectually stimulating opportunity to work with many renowned professors. Some focused on psychopharmacology, others on phenomenology, while a few had developed an expertise in psychotherapy. I learnt from all of them, but I grew particularly close to Dr. Eugene Wolf, a visiting professor of psychotherapy from England.

One day, Dr. Wolf announced a plan to offer group therapy sessions. He wanted one resident to join him as a co-therapist. Despite being the most junior resident I was the one most motivated to become a psychotherapist, so I approached Dr Wolf. To my surprise, none of the other residents showed any interest in group psychotherapy. Dr. Wolf accepted me as his assistant and I was thrilled.

I remember the first time Dr. Wolf met with the residents. He told us he had been approached by an internist to see a patient in the Intensive Care Unit who was admitted after a suicide attempt. Dr Wolf suggested that he would like to interview the patient in front of the residents. We all agreed.

After a few minutes the nurse brought in a tall, bearded, heavyset man with red hair. Dr Wolf rose, shook hands and exchanged introductions with the patient, Bill, inviting him to sit on the chair next to him. Bill looked very reserved. When Dr Wolf asked him what brought him to the hospital he shared that he was a pharmacist and had calculated the exact dose of medication required to kill himself. One afternoon, when his wife, Sheila had arranged to go away for the weekend to see her sister, he had planned to take an overdose. Sheila left at 5pm and he took the overdose at 5:30. His wife returned unexpectedly, having forgotten her purse, and found him unconscious in his bed. She called the ambulance and he was brought to the Emergency Department. His stomach was pumped and he was admitted to the Intensive Care Unit to be seen by a psychiatrist.

When Dr. Wolf asked him why he wanted to kill himself he explained that his life was a complete failure—one of the proofs he offered was that even his suicide attempt was unsuccessful. Bill told us that some people think committing suicide is an irrational act but he believed he had analyzed his life logically and his decision to kill himself was a rational choice as he had no reason to live.

When Dr. Wolf inquired about his wife, Bill stated they were married twenty years and he believed she did not love him anymore. He thought she stayed with him out of pity. She had not told him she loved him in years and they shared a sexless and loveless marriage.

At the end of the session, Dr. Wolf offered Bill a therapeutic contract. In exchange for a promise not to commit suicide for six months Dr. Wolf would see him for weekly individual, marital and group therapy sessions. Bill thought for the longest time and accepted Dr. Wolf's invitation saying, "I have to die anyhow. I can wait for another few months."

I was impressed by the way Dr. Wolf interviewed his patient, and by how he viewed Bill's agreement to six months of psychotherapy as a favour. I thought if Dr. Wolf could save his life it would be a miracle.

When I met with Dr. Wolf alone he shared his philosophy with me. He was an admirer of Harry Stack Sullivan, an American psychiatrist, and founder of interpersonal psychiatry in North America. Sullivan believed human relationships can be a source of great anxiety, depression and low self esteem, and that a caring and compassionate relationship is healing. Dr. Wolf believed people committed suicide when they lost all special connections with other human beings. Even one loving connection was enough to prevent it. Dr. Wolf planned to offer Bill a caring therapeutic relationship and explore his relationship with his wife.

As their therapy got underway, we found out more about Bill and Sheila as individuals, and the relationship they shared. Bill told us that his mother died giving birth to her second child when Bill was only two. His father remarried when he was three but his stepmother was abusive and jealous of Bill's relationship with his father. Finally, Bill was sent to live with his grandmother when he was five. His grandmother died of a stroke when he was ten and he returned to his dad and step-mom. As a teenager, he went to live in the college hostel and never went back home. Dr. Wolf thought Bill was deprived of nurturing and a mother's love. He had found refuge in rationalization and intellectualization and had difficulties connecting with others on an emotional level. He had met his wife at university and both of them enjoyed discussing philosophy and science. Their love was intellectual love.

Sheila, on the other hand, was brought up in a family where her brother had died two years before her birth. Her father wanted a son, so when Sheila was born, she was treated as a boy and developed into a tomboy. Her dad used to dress her like a boy and take her to his business meetings. Sheila became an intellectual, obtained a Masters in Science and became a Science teacher. She was a matter-of-fact person and rarely focused on her feelings. When she met Bill at university she was glad to find someone who was as interested in abstract thinking as she was.

When Dr. Wolf interviewed Sheila, she was shocked to learn that Bill believed she did not love him. When Sheila asked what she could do to help Bill, Dr Wolf suggested,

"For a few months, rather than starting your sentences with 'I think" you should start with "I feel."

He helped Sheila see that Bill needed a strong emotional connection to live and thrive. He wanted her to nurture him.

In the next few months, Dr. Wolf suggested the couple have weekly dates, go for dinners, movies, dances and plan their romantic encounters. It was amazing to see Bill change and smile and laugh and respond to Sheila emotionally and romantically.

After six months, when Dr. Wolf interviewed Bill again in front of the residents, Bill thanked him for giving him a new life. Dr Wolf believed it was not his miracle, it was the miracle of a healing relationship. After that encounter with Dr. Wolf and Bill, I wondered whether I would be able to help suicidal patients and perform such healing miracles when I became a practicing psychotherapist.

....

When the satisfaction or the security of another person becomes

as significant to one as one's own satisfaction or security, then the state of love exists. Under no other circumstances is a state of love present, regardless of the popular usage of the term. Harry Stack Sullivan

8. *LIGHT AT THE END OF THE DARK TUNNEL FROM MELANCHOLY TO DEPRESSION*

On November 13th, 2013 I was invited by Congress of Black Women to give a lecture on Depression. The essence of my lecture is as follows:

Ladies and Gentlemen,

Before I start my presentation I would like to thank Joan McLaughlin, my long term friend and colleague and Shirley Bell, the Vice President of the Congress of Black Women, for inviting me to today's meeting and giving me an opportunity to share my thoughts.

Let me start with a quotation. Robert Burton, in 1621 in his book, *The Anatomy of Melancholy,* wrote, "If there be a hell upon earth, it is to be found in a melancholy man's heart."

I am sharing this quotation to highlight not only the intensity of suffering but also how, for centuries, depression was called melancholy. The term depression became popular in the last century. Depressed people suffer not only because of their emotional pain but also because they are unable to share that pain with others.

David Foster Wallace in his short story *The Depressed Person*, published in The New Yorker in 1998, tried to capture that feeling in these words,

"The depressed person was in terrible and unceasing emotional pain, and the impossibility of sharing or articulating this pain was itself a component of the pain and a contributing factor in its essential horror."

Let me share a story of my patient Maureen so that you can appreciate the dilemmas and dynamics of people who suffer from depression. When I met Maureen she was 66. She was treated by a couple of psychiatrists, admitted to the hospital, and tried on different medications to no benefit before she came to see me.

During my assessment, I discovered that her depression had started the day when her husband, after breakfast, gave her a crumpled piece of paper. She unfolded the piece of paper and saw the statement, *'All these thirty five years of my life that I spent with you was a waste of time."* After giving her the note, her husband went to his room and picked up his suitcase.

"Don't you think we should discuss this?" Maureen asked.

He responded, "There is nothing more to discuss" and left the house never to come back.

After he left, Maureen fell apart. Her dreams of comfortable retirement and spending the golden years of her life with her husband turned into nightmares. She was heartbroken and no anti-depressants could mend her heart.

While I was helping Maureen cope with her loss and grieve a dream, I discovered that before she had met her husband she was an artist. She not only created paintings herself, she also taught art and enjoyed it.

When I suggested to Maureen that focusing on her creativity might help her recover from her depression, she did not seem very optimistic. For a while I insisted and she resisted. Finally she gave in and took out her easel and brought out her old brushes and paints. After a couple of weeks she bought new brushes and paints. I asked her to sit in front of the easel for half an hour twice a week. For the first four weeks nothing happened; then she had a visit from her muse. When she told me about her first painting I could see a twinkle in her eyes. I could see she was on the road to recovery. Rather than focusing on the sadness and anger towards her husband, she was preoccupied with the happiness and euphoria of her own creativity. She sold her first painting for $400. I invited her grown up children to see the painting. They were impressed and felt proud of their mom. Her second painting sold for $500, the third for $600 and the fourth for $700.

After a few weeks, she started connecting and meeting other artists and joined an artist's club. She met another artist and started dating. When she talked about her new love interest she blushed like a teenager. He painted watercolours and she worked in oils. They would meet and create together. They even had an exhibition together.

I am sharing this story to highlight that there is a light at the end of dark tunnel of depression. People recover and get better and transform their breakdown into a breakthrough when they get proper help and support from their friends, family members and therapists.

There has been a lot of confusion about depression because, like *love*, it is one of the most misunderstood words in the English language. Different people use the same word and mean different things. Even professionals talk and write about different types of depression in a way that confuses laypeople. In the last fifty years, some of the terms used by professionals are Neurotic Depression, Psychotic Depression, Exogenous Depression, Endogenous Depression, Uni-Polar Depression, Bipolar Depression, Primary Depression, Secondary Depression. I remember a teenager asking me a question when I was giving a lecture on mental health in a high school. He said, "When people are high we call it mania, when they are low we call it depression. Is manic depression not a contradiction in terms?" I explained that the same person can be depressed one year and manic the next year, that is why he can be suffering from manic depression.

There was a time in history when people believed that a melancholic person was possessed by ghosts and spirits. They attributed mental illness to supernatural causes. Gradually, humans began to explore natural causes of emotional problems, a process started by Greek philosophers. In 500 BC, Hippocrates, the father of medicine, presented a humoral theory. He believed that the human body had four humours: blood, phlegm, yellow bile and black bile. He believed that an increase in black bile (Greek, *melaina chole),* secreted from the spleen, was the cause of melancholy. There was a time when patients were treated with leeches and blood letting to cure their melancholia. It was not until the eighteenth century that doctors and scientists realized melancholy was related to the brain rather than the spleen.

By the nineteenth century, Emil Kraeplin had divided mental illnesses into two groups, dementia praecox, [now known as schizophrenia] and manic depression. The first related primarily to the problems of thinking, and the second to the problems of mood. In the twentieth century Adolf Meyer popularized the term Depression.

Twentieth century advances in medicine, neurology, science and psychology helped us gain a better understanding of depression. Different research workers offered different theories. We can divide those theories into three groups, beginning with biological theories.

According to biological theories, depression has genetic and biological causes. Many people suffering from Bipolar

Disorder have a family history of depression and have a biochemical imbalance in the brain, exhibiting lower levels of the neurotransmitters dopamine and serotonin.

Psychological theories, on the other hand, hold that factors in human personality and relationships contribute to depression. Sigmund Freud related depression to a strong super-ego that tries to punish the person. Edith Jacobson related depression to low self esteem, and Seligman related depression to learned helplessness. Some psychologists related depression to an idealist and perfectionist personality that has high expectations—people with obsessive compulsive personality traits get easily disappointed in themselves and life and feel depressed.

The final group encompasses social theories and highlights the many social factors that contribute to depression. People considered second class citizens in their communities because of gender, skin colour or sexual persuasion, do not enjoy equal rights. As a minority they can be more vulnerable to depression. Social theories also emphasize the family dynamics that can contribute to depression.

Because of these theories and advances, mental health professionals have adopted a bio-psycho-social model of depression and created multi-disciplinary teams to help depressed patients and their families. Today, in many hospitals we have a psychiatrist, a social worker, a nurse, a psychologist, an occupational therapist and even a minister on the team. All these professionals put their heads together to find ways to help depressed people and their families cope with depression. Each depressed person is unique. Mental health professionals and teams try to tailor therapy depending upon the needs of that person and family. Most teams offer combination therapy, a combination of medications, individual, family and group therapy, in the hospital, outpatient clinic or in the community.

The more we, as mental health professionals, understand the dynamics of depression the better we serve our patients and communities. In our Green Zone Clinic, we have developed a Green Zone Model to help our patients. The Green Zone Model is a self-help program that encourages our patients—and their family members—to understand and deal with their emotional triggers and find healthy ways to communicate with each other. Our book, *Green Zone Living,* discusses seven steps to helping people create a healthy, happy and peaceful lifestyle. Green Zone Philosophy focuses on mental health education as we believe in empowerment through learning.

Thank you for listening to my reflections on Melancholy and Depression.

9.   *THE LAST HOPE*

Yesterday was Saturday, and every other Saturday I go to my Creative Psychotherapy Clinic to see three or four patients. Yesterday, after I saw two patients, my secretary asked me to listen to a message that one of my patients, J, had left on our answering machine. It said,

"Dr. Sohail, I am feeling depressed. I have no reason to live. I want to commit suicide."

I had not seen J for nearly three months. The last time we met I had given him a referral letter for admission to hospital. He was feeling depressed and was contemplating suicide. After that meeting I had not seen or talked to him.

I thought about the message for a while and then I called 911. I shared my concerns about my patient and gave the operator his address and phone number so the police could see if he was okay.

After some minutes, the police department called me and requested I meet them at my patient's house in Pickering, twenty minutes from my Whitby clinic. While I was driving there I reflected on J's life. He was once a very successful man. A scientist and an artist, he was a professional engineer as well as an opera singer. He led a very successful life. But he became physically and mentally unwell. He became diabetic and following his retirement he became depressed, gradually losing touch with his family and friends. When I first met him he was unhappily married and struggling financially. Then his wife left him and he fell apart. He could not look after himself and went rapidly downhill.

He attended our clinic for a few months but it became more and more difficult as he had a hard time coming down the stairs. I suggested that if he could not live alone, he could connect with Community Mental Health Services who could arrange a residence for him where he would be looked after and supervised by the staff. I gave him the name and number of a social worker but he was not inclined to contact them, preferring instead to live alone. He had difficulty looking after himself. He did not take his medications regularly and his health began to deteriorate further. Incontinence, resulting from his diabetes, made him withdrawn. It was sad to see him regress step by step. Three months ago I had referred him back to his family doctor with a number of recommendations.

When I reached his street I could not find his house so I went to the Pickering Police Station. The officer told me he had moved and gave me the new address. Upon arriving at the new address I saw three police officers waiting for me. J was living in a tiny room in a very rundown house. It seemed like part of a slum. When I entered J's room I was shocked. It was filthy. There were dozens of dirty bags full of things that seemed like garbage. The room appeared not to have been cleaned in months. J sat on a stool looking pale and weak. His clothes were dirty, I could see his trousers were soiled, and it was obvious he had not showered in weeks. Finding nowhere to sit down, I sat on the floor in front to him to talk to him. He told me that the night before he had felt desperate and wanted to end his life. His last hope was me, so he called and left the message. He was lost and confused and did not know what to do with his life. He had no meaning or reason to live.

I told him I felt very concerned after I heard his message. That is why I called the police and came to help him. I asked him to cooperate with me and accompany the police officers to the hospital. He reflected on my suggestion for a few seconds and then agreed. I asked him to get ready. When I told the police officers that J was willing to go to the hospital they asked if I was going to sign Form One for his involuntary admission. I shared that the reason I drove there was to request J to voluntarily be admitted. I did not sign Form One—it was humiliating for a patient to be handcuffed in order to be taken to the hospital. The police officers called for an ambulance and asked me if I would go with them to the Emergency Department of the Pickering Hospital. Their concern was that if I did not sign Form One and did not go with them, the Emergency staff would make them wait for hours and might not even admit J. I agreed to accompany them.

Arriving at the hospital, I found a police officer waiting for me. I spoke with the doctor on duty in the emergency department, introducing myself as Dr Sohail, a psychiatrist, who had known J for a while. I told the doctor that he was depressed and suicidal and unable to look after himself. He needed hospitalization and professional help in a supervised group home to recover and live. The doctor on duty was very sympathetic and reassured me that when J was brought by the ambulance he would be admitted to the psychiatric floor.

As I prepared to leave the hospital the police officer thanked me for cooperating with them and I thanked the officer for helping me get J the help he needed. I did not want anyone to find his dead body in his room.

Driving back to my clinic, I was pleased that we saved a depressed man who had given up on life. I was his last hope and I had wanted to respond to his existential crisis. I wanted him to know that someone cared whether he lived or killed himself. I was impressed by the cooperation of the police officers and the doctor on duty. It was good teamwork and I was glad to be a part of a team that was serving humanity by serving the community.

I wonder about all the men and women who live like islands in our communities, feeling depressed and desperate, gradually running out of hope. Who will answer their call?
March 2014

10.   THREE HOURS IN COURT

The first time I met Connie in the admitting department of Whitby Psychiatric Hospital she looked sad. Connie was a twenty-five year-old single mother. When she showed me the picture of Celine, her four-year-old daughter, she had tears in her eyes. She had been depressed for the last few months because the Children's Aid Society [CAS] of Quebec was refusing to give Celine back to her.

When I asked the details I found out that Connie had struggled with drug addiction when she was in Montreal. Before entering a Drug Rehab Program she took her daughter to CAS and asked them to look after her while she received her treatment. She willingly signed the papers they gave her because she wanted to cooperate with the authorities. After a few weeks of treatment, when she was discharged from the Rehab Program she went back to CAS to get her daughter but they refused to relinquish Celine into her care, telling her she had given them permanent custody. It was then that she discovered she had been deceived when she signed the papers in French. She thought she was signing temporary custody but in reality she had signed permanent custody and CAS had declared her an unfit and incompetent mother.

Connie had moved to Ontario to be with her cousin who was supportive of her. When Connie asked for my help I wrote a letter to the judge in Montreal asking him to transfer her daughter to Ontario so she could fight her case here. The judge honoured my request and transferred Celine's case to CAS in Ontario. Connie applied to Oshawa Court to get her daughter back but CAS refused.

One day, I received a call from Connie's lawyer to discuss her case. I had sent him a letter of support. He thanked me for the letter but told me that CAS is very strong and would not relinquish her daughter. He advised I appear in court and personally fight for my patient and convince the judge. His request inspired me. As a teenager I had dreamed of becoming a lawyer, I thought I could fulfill that dream for one day by being an advocate for my patient.

At court, I was kept on the stand for three hours. It was one of the most incredible experiences of my life.

The case started with an ethical dilemma, when I refused

to put my hand on the Bible. The judge asked me if I wanted the Quran. I told him,

"I believe in neither the Bible nor the Quran because I am a humanist."

"What is sacred for you?"

"My conscience," I answered.

" So take an oath on your conscience."

And I did.

That afternoon I was interrogated by three lawyers, Connie's lawyer, Celine's lawyer and, most aggressively of all, by the CAS lawyer, Ms Fergusan, who was very unsympathetic to my patient. She argued that Connie was a drug addict who had just come out of Rehab Program and could not be trusted as a mother. My position was that she was a responsible woman who got professional help and was motivated to be a good mother and that we should offer her all the support she needed. I believed that a sympathetic approach would be more effective than a punitive one and we should not punish her by taking her daughter away from her.

When Ms Fergusan criticized my patient for not attending some of her appointments I reacted strongly.

"You are being unfair. For middle class professionals to buy a two-dollar ticket might not be an issue, but for a single mother, two dollars for a one-way bus ticket is a lot of money. She gets $540 from Social Services, out of which she pays $440 in rent, and from the remaining $100 she must buy food and clothes for herself and her daughter. Social Services do not refund her bus fare, so we need to be careful before we criticize Connie".

When Ms Fergusan accused me of irresponsibility in transferring the girl from Quebec to Ontario, the judge stopped her.

"I usually keep quiet but in this instance I must speak. Ms Fergusan, it was not Dr Sohail who transferred Celine to Ontario. It was done by the judge's order from Montreal. Dr Sohail submitted a request to the judge and the judge accepted his recommendation. Dr Sohail did what any good psychiatrist would do for his patient."

At the end of the trial the judge accepted my recommendation and ordered the little girl to be returned to her mother's custody. I felt pleased when my patient thanked me and when her lawyer told me he would not have won the case without me. The only person who was in a bad mood was Ms Ferguson.

That day I learned I might have been a good lawyer had I chosen that profession. Fighting for human rights and for the underdog has been my lifelong passion as a poet, humanist and a psychotherapist.

11. DEVELOPING A COMMUNITY MENTAL HEALTH PROGRAM

I remember that April day in 1984 when Dr Don Wasalenki, the psychiatrist-in-chief, invited me to his office and said, "Dr. Sohail, although you have been working in this hospital for a just few weeks you have already become quite popular among other doctors, nurses and social workers. We have decided to re-organize the hospital and we are starting a new Admissions Department. We want all patients to be assessed before they are admitted, and we want you to be in charge of this new department."

I smiled.

"Dr. Wasalenki, I feel honoured but also surprised. There are so many senior psychiatrists in this hospital who have been working here for years, even decades. Rather than choosing one of them, why are you choosing me?'

"To be in charge of the Admissions Department" he explained, "you not only have to be a good psychiatrist, you also need to be good in public relationships. You will be dealing with the staff of ten hospitals, all bringing their patients for assessment. We will also be working with police officers, ambulance workers and family members. There will be times when you have to say NO to them and deal with their negative reactions. We think you are the only psychiatrist in the hospital who can do that well."

"I take that as a compliment. Thank you for trusting me with that responsibility. But I have a request."

"What is that?" Dr. Wasalenki was curious.

"If you are giving me the responsibility, you also need to give me authority to choose my team of a nurse and a social worker who would enjoy working with me. I will produce better results if I like, and get along with, members of my team."

"No problem."

I accepted responsibility for the creation of a new team and began constructing a new Admissions Department within the Whitby Psychiatric Hospital in 1984. Of the new team, the staff members who became most important to me were the Community Mental Health Nurse, Anne Aguirre and Hildy Abrams, the social worker. Not only were we colleagues but also firm friends.

In August 1984, we began assessing and admitting patients. My title was Admitting Doctor but I tried my best not to admit people. I wanted to make admission to a psychiatric hospital difficult because I believed in community mental health care rather than institutional care. But to do that, we needed to accurately assess the needs of our patients and their families and be able to provide alternate care. In the past, when a person's behaviour became bizarre or inappropriate, their relatives approached the family doctor. The GP signed a Form 1 ordering the patient involuntary admission to Whitby Psychiatric Hospital for 120 hours, for psychiatric assessment. I believed this was unfair to patients and violated their human rights.

In the beginning, when I assessed a patient within the space of an hour and declared admission unnecessary, that they could be helped and treated as an outpatient, the family members, family physicians, police officers and ambulance drivers were all upset. They were used to bringing the patients and leaving them—effectively dumping them—in the hospital. I asked them to wait until the assessment was complete and, if the patient was not admitted, to take them back to their homes. To change their attitudes I had to do a lot of mental health education and explain to them that Form 1 only assured psychiatric assessment—it could be done in one hour or could take *up to* 120 hours. There were some tense moments when I did not admit the patient, but I stood firm. I was on the side of patients and their human rights rather than the convenience of relatives or staff. I was lucky to have the assistance of Dr. Wasalenki who always supported my decisions. I was also very fortunate to have staff who were efficient, cooperative and respectful. Our team, the Admissions Team, was called 'the A Team' and had the highest morale in the hospital.

After a few months of working in the Admissions Department, I had a special meeting with Dr. Wasalenki. I informed him there were nearly 1600 admissions to our hospital every year. It was my estimation that half of them were unecessary if we could arrange alternate care.

"What do you suggest? Dr Wasalenki asked.

"We need clinics in the community and a boarding home that will help with patients in crisis."

Dr Wasalenki agreed with my suggestions. He organized community clinics in Ajax, Whitby, Bowmanville, even Lindsay, over seventy kilometres northeast of us. In the meantime Dr Arfai joined our hospital and became Head of the Community Mental Health Department. We hired more staff, including Norma Semple and Lisa Bishop as nurses and David Seale and Bob Falconer as social workers. Lisa Bishop and I used to make the hour's drive to Lindsay to run a weekly clinic.

With the help of Hildy Abrams, our social worker, I met with a boarding home operator in Whitby. We explained how sometimes, on Friday afternoons, patients arrive at the hospital in a state of emotional crisis because of marital or family conflict with no neutral place to stay for the weekend. Rather than admitting them to a psychiatric hospital we preferred they stay in a boarding home. The operator told us she charged eleven dollars per night. A whole month was three-hundred dollars. We met with a social worker from the Social Services Department and explained that a single patient admission costs the government nearly four-hundred dollars a night. If we sent them to a boarding home it would cost only thirty-three dollars for the weekend. If patients could afford to, they would pay the landlady from their own pocket, if not we would ask Social Services to pay the thirty-three dollars. The social worker agreed. I had another meeting with Dr. Wasalenki and shared my plan of action. He was impressed.

In the next ten years we developed a Community Mental Health Program that sought to treat people in Community Clinics and, if they were in a crisis, we had the option of a boarding home rather than admit them to a psychiatric hospital. That arrangement improved the quality of patient care for many, including the homeless and those dependent on the welfare system.

With the new plan in place, admissions to the hospital started decreasing. Each year the number dropped by nearly one hundred. From 1,600 admissions per year in 1984 when I started working there, it came down to 756 in 1995 when I left the hospital to start my own Creative Psychotherapy Clinic with Anne Aguirre. Working in Whitby Psychiatric Hospital and taking part in the development of the Community Mental health Service with the help of Dr Wasalenki, Dr Arfai and the various nurses and social workers was a great learning experience for me. It highlighted how psychiatric patients were expected to deal with multiple agencies, and to improve the standard of care for them we needed to train and educate the staff, change people's attitudes and develop programs that were compassionate and humane. I learnt that patients, their families, their doctors, hospitals, social services and the government were all part of a larger picture, and to provide better care for the mentally ill and homeless we needed wise leaders capable of developing a caring and compassionate program that fostered cooperation between agencies and team members. We developed an attitude that people suffering from emotional and social problems were at the centre of the services and staff members used their abilities to serve them. It was there I learnt that serving the mentally ill was an honour and I felt lucky to have the opportunity to assist the sick, the poor and the homeless with dignity, respecting their human rights. I still meet some of those patients in downtown Whitby, their reciprocal respect and regard for me is evident in their warm greetings.

12.   CREATING A MEANINGFUL LIFE

In the last few years a number of people struggling emotionally have come to my clinic to consult me as a psychotherapist. They did not suffer from any mental illness. They were not psychotic or clinically depressed. Their main complaint was:

"My life is meaningless."

"I have no purpose in life."

"My life is not fulfilling."

While working with these people in therapy, I prepared a questionnaire to send to my friends and colleagues, exploring how they found meaning in their lives. I thought their responses could help my patients discover their own personal sense of meaning. Included were the following four questions:

1.   *Do you believe LIFE has a meaning? If yes, what is it?*
2.   *Does YOUR LIFE have meaning? If yes, what makes it meaningful?*
3.   *Did you ever feel YOUR LIFE was meaningless? If yes, how did you make it meaningful?*
4.   *Do you consider yourself a religious, spiritual or a secular person? What is your philosophy of life?*

I was pleasantly surprised by the enthusiastic responses, which ranged in length from five lines, to five paragraphs, to five pages. Interestingly, among the respondents there were more men than women and more secular than religious people. The resulting answers could be divided into the following groups:

1. MEANINGFUL PERSONAL DREAMS

A number of respondents had personal goals, ambitions and dreams that gave them a sense of meaning. Following their passions and dreams made them feel positive and their lives more enjoyable. Some wanted to attain their fullest potential, while others wanted to develop their artistic talents and create masterpieces.

One respondent said, "One must live one's life to the fullest…ensuring one is true to oneself first and foremost…"

One artist responded, "Until I have created my 'masterpiece' there will be a void, but perhaps that is the pursuit of many artists."

A writer stated, "I read books, I write books, which makes life very meaningful."

One respondent quoted George Eliot who said, "It is never too late to become what you might have been."

2. MEANINGFUL RELATIONSHIPS

A number of respondents found meaning in their emotional bonds. For them, their friends, sweethearts, spouses, colleagues and relatives enriched their lives; their loving relationships gave them meaning. One mother said, "My children make my life meaningful…"

Another respondent stated, "What makes life meaningful is the fact that I have a family, have children, grandchildren, friends, relatives…."

3. MEANINGFUL SERVICE TO HUMANITY

A large number of respondents believed serving other human beings made their lives meaningful. Their altruistic behaviour helped them transcend an individual mindset and made them feel part of humanity, where they played a role in creating a happy, healthy and peaceful world. One respondent said, "My life has meaning because I care about other human beings. I have been involved in human rights issues since I was a teenager and I have been trying to educate people about that. Another task that I have taken upon myself is to encourage people to adopt scientific thinking and I have been quite successful in that. Those endeavours make my life meaningful. They make me feel that I HAVE made a difference."

4. MEANINGFUL CONNECTION WITH GOD AND RELIGION

A small number of respondents felt a special relationship with their God and religion gave meaning to their lives. One respondent, who suffered from depression, felt religious belief helped many depressed people—desperate enough to have otherwise committed suicide—stay alive. He stated, " …in the case of depression, it is religion that gives you support and a light for living, otherwise there should have been many more suicides in the world than those occurring at present. Everyone gets depression at one time or another. Some overcome it without any help, some need psychiatric help. Religion, right or wrong, provides a good psychiatric support to overcome depression and provides a meaning to life and urge to live." One female Muslim stated, "I have always felt the presence of Allah around me and that has always been meaningful to me."

Another male Muslim wrote, "So I am a Muslim and believe in One God, the Creator and the concept of life after death and accountability of my actions in this existing life. And this assumption or faith has made my life meaningful."

DOES LIFE IN GENERAL HAVE MEANING?

In my interviews, alongside asking people about their personal lives, I also asked them whether life in general had a meaning. Most secular people believed life had no intrinsic meaning while spiritual and religious people believed life had an inherent meaning. Some seemed unsure. One woman said, "Life has a meaning but I do not know what it is." Some believed it SHOULD have a meaning otherwise life would be meaningless and the idea of a meaningless life made them uncomfortable. One respondent stated, "Every life must have had a meaning, for if not, then the whole act of creation becomes meaningless..."

It was interesting to see how, for some religious people faith in God and religion made their lives meaningful, while for spiritual people it was their spiritual ideals. One Muslim stated, "My life has a meaning to serve Allah and be able to connect people with Allah." On the other hand, secular people did not need God, religion or spiritual values to make their lives meaningful. For them art, music, loving relationships and serving humanity were enough to create an enjoyable, exciting and meaningful life. For some secular people, spirituality was more connected with humanity than divinity. One secular respondent said, "I am a very spiritual and secular humanist. The source of spirituality is love, knowledge and above all music."

Some secular people had a unique perspective on the meaninglessness of life. One stated, "I find meaningfulness of life in its meaninglessness." Another non-religious person felt meaning was not important to enjoy life. He said, " ...overall I find my life most satisfying—whether with or without meaning." Others believed that as human beings evolve and develop their rational and logical thinking, their need for God and organized religion will lessen. One respondent stated, "God was created by humans for psychological and emotional reasons. As human courage and wisdom grows further, God will be buried in the caves he came from"

It was fascinating to see how secular people searched for meaning in life without religious and spiritual traditions. One quoted Bertrand Russell for defining good life, "A good life is one, inspired by love and guided by knowledge." Another responded that he tried to make his life meaningful by, "enjoying various thrills of life that nature has gifted us, with the least amount of guilt and repentance." He added, "I am extraordinarily conscious of my cosmic ignorance and I strive to be compassionately ego-less, carefully fearless and ethically guilt-free.".

SERVING HUMANITY

Despite their differences of opinion, the respondents reached a consensus on one aspect. Most agreed that serving humanity was a major source of meaning in life, connecting them with other human beings in a meaningful way.

One respondent said, "...one of the major pleasures is to be of some help to other human beings..." Such behaviours decrease human suffering and increase quality of life, creating genuine bonds between people that transcend religious, cultural, gender and ethnic differences. It it as though, by serving humanity, human beings can strive to become fully human individually and collectively, rise to the next stage of human evolution and participate in creating a loving, just and peaceful world. One of my favourite responses claimed, "My aim is to be the best person I can be and to strive to change the world for the better even in a small way."

Reviewing the responses, I realized some people had accepted the traditional meaning of life, the meaning offered to them by their families, communities, religions and cultures, while others had rejected the traditional meaning and found their own instead.

When I shared these responses with the patients in my clinic who were struggling with meaninglessness in their lives, they found them helpful. They offered hope and inspired them to discover their own unique meaning by:

...focusing on their personal talents and pursuing a hobby, a passion and a dream. They finally got in touch with the special

gift life offered them they had thus far been unaware of,
...developing new relationships and creating a circle of close friends that I call *family of the heart*
and
...doing some voluntary work to serve their communities.

I was pleased my friends sent such thoughtful answers to my questions and felt honoured that my patients gave me an opportunity to help them in creating meaningful lives, consequently giving meaning to my life as a humanist psychotherapist.

PART THREE

Creative Essays

13. FROM CREATIVE RAIN TO CREATIVE SPRING

There was a time when I used to experience creative rain. I would write a poem, a short story or an essay and this would be followed by a long dry period. But in the last few years the rain has transformed into a spring. That spring keeps on flowing day and night, weekdays and weekends. I no longer experience 'writer's block'. Such a transformation took place after I became aware that although the creative process is related to our unconscious, we can yet learn to influence and guide it. I have read about psychotherapy patients who remembered their dreams regularly because they kept a daily dream diary to share them with their analysts. I thought, if people could learn to have more control of their dreams then why could I not influence my own creative process, as they both originate from the same springs of the unconscious mind? Over the years my muse and I became friends and started creating together. That is why my creative output has increased over the years.

My creative journey has become a part of my self-discovery, self-awareness and self-actualization. I believe my creativity has helped me liberate myself and discover an adventurous lifestyle. It has made me become a better friend, a more caring therapist and a happier human being, during which time I have learnt a few things about myself.

CREATIVE MORNINGS

Mornings are the best time for me to write and create. I always have blank pages, pens and pencils lying next to my bed. I think about the project I am working on the night before, and when I wake up I am ready to write. It seems as if my muse, my dear friend, is active even when I am sleeping. Like a research assistant, she goes into the deep recesses of my past and collects all the relevant thoughts, ideas, images and references and then offers her significant homework in the morning as my creative breakfast. The last article I wrote was about one of my favourite writers, Anais Nin. When my friend Rashid Mughal, who also loves the writings of Anais Nin, asked me to share my impressions about Nin, I became inspired to write an essay about her life and philosophy. I thought about her diaries and interviews all evening before I went to bed. In the morning, when I awoke and started writing, it was like a stream of consciousness and I was surprised to write nearly ten pages spontaneously. Afterwards I consulted her diaries, lectures and interviews and added a few quotations to highlight my points. The whole process was so enjoyable. I was quite amused by Nin's relationship to creativity as it seemed so similar to mine. I could identify with her, when she wrote,' The white page for me is like a ski slope. I go absolutely mad. I go mad in stationary stores. Just to see beautiful paper gives me a desire to write.'

In the morning I feel as if my mind is like a blank page, ready to receive the mysterious gifts from the right side of my brain, from my unconscious mind, from my creative self, from my muse.

CREATIVE PROJECTS

I like working on different projects at the same time, so that when I get tired or bored with one I can turn to another with renewed energy. These days I am working on the following projects:

a) proofreading my book, *The Myth of the Chosen One*, which focuses on the psychology of serial killers and mass murderers.

b) researching material for my book *Prophets of Violence, Prophets of Peace,* focusing on the struggles of reformers and revolutionaries. I want to read the biographies of Tolstoy, Gandhi, Martin Luther King and Nelson Mandela, who I consider the four messengers of Peace and Justice in the twentieth century. I chose these four when I realized that Gandhi, as a teenager, was impressed by Tolstoy. He used to write to him and read his books for inspiration. He inspired people around the world when he introduced his philosophy of non-violence in India. One of those people was Martin Luther King. Later on, Martin Luther King inspired Nelson Mandela. When I read the Nobel speech of Nelson Mandela, I was touched to read his compliments to Martin Luther King. It was also interesting to learn that before Gandhi started his struggle in India against the British Empire, he had lived in South Africa and was influenced by the struggles of Asians there. Reading about those personalities will keep my creative juices flowing for a few months until I finish that project.

c) I am also trying to finalize my book, *The Art of Living in your Green Zone*, based on my twenty-five years of experience as a psychotherapist. In that book I will discuss the new concepts I have developed in my clinical practice.

CREATIVE TRANSLATIONS

To improve my craft and the art of writing, I became involved in translating world literature into Urdu. To do that I have to read the classics a few times and get in touch with the soul of the writers. Such translations inspire me with my own creative work. During translations, if I am inspired to write something of my own I put the translations on hold and do my own creative work. I can always come back to the translations, but I may not be able to catch the creative moment later on.

My last project on translations was about Native Indian Literature. When Asif Furrukhi, a well-respected writer and editor from Pakistan, was visiting Canada, I shared with him the translation of Chief Seattle's speech. He was so impressed by the translation and the speech, he asked me if I would consider doing some more translations. He told me that writers in Pakistan had translated European, Middle Eastern and South American literature into Urdu but nobody had translated Native Indian Literature. I promised to do that and completed the project in a few months.

CREATIVE FRIENDS

Over the years, I have developed friendships with creative people all over the world. I call them the family of my heart. After finishing my first drafts, I share my creative products with these friends via email. They are very thoughtful and send me their sincere and honest comments and suggestions that help me in finalizing the draft. I am lucky to have a number of such friends who are co-travellers on my creative journey. They feel that writing and commenting on my creations inspires them to complete their own creative projects.

I am usually involved in joint projects, as I believe that one and one make eleven—in creative friendships people bring out the best in each other.
I am lucky to work with Anne Henderson who is not only a wonderful nurse but also a sincere friend. We have intellectually stimulating discussions at lunch on a regular basis. My dialogues with Anne have helped me formulate and articulate my philosophy.

CREATIVE HOLIDAYS

After a few weeks of working in my clinic and leading a routine life, I take a week off to visit my creative friends and complete my unfinished projects. When I leave home to go on a trip, I get a creative boost. My creative juices start flowing with more enthusiasm. While I am at the airport, or in the plane or visiting friends in distant lands, or sitting on a beach on an island, I can review the last few weeks and plan the next few weeks. Such a review is like a landing space after going upstairs. After an upward climb we need a little rest, to recover and to regain our energy. I have realized that the creative journey is like running a marathon and this is why I use turtles as a metaphor in my practice. They are slow, but they travel long distances, live long lives and become successful in the end. Fast runners like the hare usually fall asleep, lose interest and lose the race. I was always more impressed by those artists who received recognition for their life-long achievements rather than a one-time performance. Serious writers in any field do not just leave one or two creative products behind, they are known for their body of work.

CREATIVE INTEGRATION

I have begun to realize my personal, social and professional lives are increasingly integrated. I am as eager to write about my professional experiences, as I am excited to share my personal encounters. It is also amazing that after creating collections of poems, stories and essays, these days I am enthused to write in the form of letters. Writing letters to friends on serious subjects is my newest form of expression and I think it is the most spontaneous. I feel at home. It gives me an opportunity to be fully myself. I find it the best combination of form and content that suits my personality and temperament. Reading diaries of Anais Nin and letters of Vincent van Gogh have made me realize that diaries and letters deserve as much serious attention in literature as poems, short stories and novels.

WRITING

The more I write, the more I discover myself,
The more I discover myself, the more I share,
The more I share, the more I connect with others in a
meaningful way,
The more I connect with others in a meaningful way, the more I
discover the secrets of making creative friends,
The more I discover the secrets of making creative friends, the
more I learn the art of growing together,
The more I learn the art of growing together, the more I feel
optimistic that our tomorrows will be more meaningful and
productive than our yesterdays.
I feel so fortunate that my creative rain transformed into a
creative spring. I hope it keeps on flowing till the day I die and
my creations inspire others to get in touch with their own
creative selves, creative springs and creative truths.

March 2002

14.   CREATIVE MISCARRIAGES

Whenever I think of creative miscarriages, I remember a poet I met in Abu Dhabi in 1984. After listening to his beautiful poems, I asked him why he had not published a collection of his poetry. He said he had only sixty poems so far—he would publish his collection when he had one hundred. I liked his poems and looked forward to the day I could buy and read his collection. After twenty years, I met him again in 2004, this time in New York. I asked him the same question and he gave me the same answer. In those twenty years he had written as many new poems as he had discarded old ones. He still had only sixty chosen poems and was waiting for the other forty. Now, I wondered if he would ever publish his poems.

In more than two decades, I have met many people with creative personalities—poets, painters, writers, film makers, scholars and philosophers—who are gestating a new idea (or a new project) but before their creative pregnancy reaches full term, they suffer a creative miscarriage or abort their pregnancy. After a while they once again become pregnant with an idea and after a few weeks or months, they have another miscarriage. Over the years they end up with a series of miscarriages. They never complete, nor do they share, their creations or products with the world. Their unborn babies and incomplete manuscripts remain hidden in drawers and closets and basements. Some of those creative personalities attain menopause without publishing a single book or producing a single film.

I have interviewed many such writers and artists over the years and asked them the reasons for their creative miscarriages and abortions. They offer a variety of reasons which can be divided into the following groups.

The first group consisted of those writers and artists who considered themselves lazy and disorganized. They started a poem, a story or an essay but then got distracted by their day-to-day responsibilities of work or family and never went back to complete their creative product. They had a big collection of first drafts none of which reached the stage of final draft. Some of them even lost many of their first drafts. It was interesting for me that many of them were not even distressed about the situation as they considered themselves *amateur* writers and artists. Their identity was connected with their profession and family. Creative identity never became their primary identity.

The second group consisted of those writers and artists who felt that their creative products were "not good enough." They did not share their creations with others as they were not satisfied with the quality of their creativity.

The third group included those who were extremely sensitive to other people's reactions and opinions. They were always worried about "what will *they* say?" Their anxiety of other people's negative judgments made them so paralyzed they couldn't bring their ideas to fruition.

The fourth group believed they changed their opinions every few years. They felt they would be embarrassed to tell people that they did not believe in their own creative ideas anymore.

The fifth group included those creative personalities who wouldn't complete their creative projects because they didn't know what to do with them after completion. They did not know a publisher who would publish their book or a producer who would release their film. They did not finish their creations because they did not want them to languish in their basements. Lack of self-confidence or networking resources was reason enough for them to freeze their creative fetuses as stillborns.

As a psychotherapist, when I listen to these reasons I often wonder if they are *real* reasons offered by creative personalities or whether they are merely justifications and rationalizations resulting from deeper psychological issues and unresolved emotional conflicts.

When I worked with such creative personalities in my clinical practice I came to know some who struggled with low self-esteem. They felt they were "not good enough" as human beings. No wonder they felt that their creations were also "not good enough". In therapy, as their self-esteem improved, their satisfaction with their creative productivity also improved. Some of the writers and artists who used to feel embarrassed by their creations became proud of their creative products and finally celebrated their creative success.

For others, it was a struggle with their obsessive compulsive personality. They were idealistic perfectionists to the nth degree. When I studied their childhoods I discovered they were brought up in families and schools where their parents and teachers had high standards and even higher expectations.

Gradually, they had internalized those high standards and judged themselves and their creations harshly. In therapy such creative personalities learnt to become realistic rather than idealistic and learnt to accept rather than judge themselves. The more they could accept themselves the more they could cherish their creations and proudly share their creative offerings with others. The more they adopted realistic standards the more they enjoyed the creative process that led them to complete their creative endeavours.

As a writer and a psychotherapist I think creative children need to be nurtured rather than judged and their creative products cherished rather than criticized. Children express their creativity by playing with toys and if their creativity is nurtured then they learn to play with words and sounds and colours and images and ideas and become poets and painters, writers and scholars, filmmakers and philosophers. If they feel good about themselves and proud of their creations they carry their creative pregnancies to full-term and deliver their masterpieces to be shared with the world. Such writers and artists are a source of entertainment as well as enlightenment for their communities and humanity as a whole Their creative products are their special gifts to the world.

August 2013

15. STORY TELLING AND STORY WRITING PRESENTED AT WRITERS FORUM MEETING TORONTO

Dear Friends,

Canadian writers are ecstatic because Alice Munroe, a Canadian short story writer, received the Nobel Prize for Literature this year. It is a great honour for Canada and Canadians. Since she is a writer who has been creating short stories for more than half of a century, many writers are reflecting on the art and craft of the short story, and since Munir Saami invited me to say a few words in the Writers' Forum Meeting, I would like to share some of my random thoughts about storytelling and story writing.

There are short stories that one can finish reading in one sitting with one theme and one focus, and there are long stories with multiple themes that need many sittings to finish. There are short, short stories and there are long, long stories. There are interesting stories and there are boring stories. There are inspiring stories and there are depressing stories. I have read hundreds of stories and written dozens of stories in my lifetime. The shortest story I read was only two lines.

Khalil Gibran wrote,

"A woman was sitting between two men.
Her one cheek was pink, the other pale."

There was a time people enjoyed listening to stories more than reading them. There were more storytellers than story writers. Those storytellers were a great source of entertainment, inspiration and enlightenment. I grew up in Peshawar, Pakistan where they had a *Qissa Khani* Bazaar [Storyteller's bazaar] where storytellers used to sip *qahva,* the green tea, and tell stories to travellers who journeyed to different countries.

Let me share one of my poems highlighting that tradition. It is titled,

A STORY TELLER

Dear Friends!
Every night

Deep Love

when it gets dark
and children go to sleep
birds hide in their nests
and
the sun travels to the other world
you people come here
and sit in a circle
in front of the fireplace
under a starry sky
sipping tea
smoking your sacred pipes
asking me to tell you a story
and I being a storyteller
who loves to tell stories
share with you
stories that I read
when I was a young boy
stories that were told to me
when I traveled to distant lands
and stories I heard from my grandmother
stories that she had heard from her grandmother
stories that have been traveling
from one heart to another
from one generation to another
as sacred wisdom and folktales
those are the stories
created and shared by our ancestors
when there were no books and radios and televisions and
internet

I have been sharing with you
every night
stories within stories
stories born from the womb of life
stories of old and young
men and women
warriors and hunters
kings and slaves
gods and goddesses

Dr. K Sohail

saints and sinners
and you listen to them attentively
but when the moon hides behind the cloud
and the stars look tired
and the sacred pipes become cold
then we all go to sleep
knowing very well that
some of you will travel
the next day
to unknown destinations
and some will come back
the next night
to listen to more stories

I was always fascinated by storytellers. In Europe and North America, after the introduction of the printing press, short story writing became more popular. But there are still many communities and cultures in Asia and Africa where the majority of the population cannot read or write and there are no newspapers and magazines, books and printing presses. The people still rely on oral tradition, a tradition that passes on the wisdom of one generation to the next, by storytelling rather than story writing.

In the tradition of Urdu short story writing, writers that rose to prominence in the first half of the twentieth century included Prem Chand and Saadat Hasan Manto, Ismat Chughtai and Rajendar Singh Bedi. These Urdu writers were similar to Anton Chekhov in Russia and Guy de Maupassant in Europe. They wrote stories with a hero, a plot, a beginning, a middle, and a sharp end with an unexpected, powerful climax. Many of those stories were based in social realism. The Progressive Writers Movement promoted such stories as powerful encouragement for societal change. But in the second half of the twentieth century, short story writing took a more modernist approach. Writers like Rasheed Amjad, Muzhar ul Islam, Anwar Sajjad and Intezar Hussain were influenced by the likes of Franz Kafka, Virginia Woolf and James Joyce. Many modern short story writers followed the stream of consciousness style. Many of their stories did not give names to their characters, some did not even have human characters, some did not have a plot, some did not have a beginning, middle or an unexpected end. Those stories were mysterious. Some looked more like prose poems than stories.

One of my favourite short story writers is Yiddish Nobel Prize Winner Isaac Singer. In one of his stories, *A Friend of Kafka,* someone criticizes Kafka for writing *The Castle* and breaking the rules of story writing. The friend says, "A master does not have to follow the rules." There are benefits to beginners in following rules but some writers reach a stage of confidence and maturity where the creative process guides them like love. Khalil Gibran said, 'Do not think you can guide love, if love finds you worthy she will guide you.' For them, writing becomes love-making. It is where art transcends craft. Kafka used to say that a good short story is the one that forces the reader to re-read the story.

The short story form evolved from the social realism of Maupassant into the magical realism of Gabriel García Márquez. And then there are short story writers like Jorge Luis Borges in whose work story and essay embrace each other. There were times I felt that South Asian Urdu short story writers might be closer to Latin American and South American writers in their essence than European writers. In Pakistan, writers like Sagheer Malal translated many Latin and South American writers into Urdu.

The twentieth century also saw a number of immigrant writers become famous. Living in two cultures, two languages, two religions and two traditions opened their third eye and they created masterpieces.

When I read short stories, I sense the invisible threads connecting to the tradition of short story writing, the evolution of language, the socio-cultural environment and the life struggles of the writer. There are many writers who base their fiction on their biography; we call it bio-fiction.

There are full time writers who write novels and there are part time writers who write short stories. And there are short story writers who wish they were novelists but cannot afford to be as they do not have the time and resources to dedicate to their art and craft. Alice Munroe writes,

"So why do I like to write short stories? Well, I certainly didn't intend to. I was going to write a novel. And still! I still come up with ideas for novels. And I even start novels. But something happens to

them. They break up. I look at what I really want to do with the material, and it never turns out to be a novel. But when I was younger, it was simply a matter of expediency. I had small children, I didn't have any help. Some of this was before the days of automatic washing machines, if you can actually believe it. There was no way I could get that kind of time. I couldn't look ahead and say, this is going to take me a year, because I thought every moment something might happen that would take all time away from me. So I wrote in bits and pieces with a limited time expectation. Perhaps I got used to thinking of my material in terms of things that worked that way."
Speaking with *The Atlantic's* Cara Feinberg in 2001

Erica Jong used to say, 'Writing a poem is like having a one night stand, writing a short story is like having an affair and writing a novel is like getting married." Different people have different tastes and express their love for life and creativity in different ways.
These are some of my serious random thoughts about storytelling and story writing. In the end, let me share a humorous dialogue between two writers.
'What are the essential ingredients of a good short story?'
'A good short story needs three elements: a little bit of sex, a little bit of religion and a little bit of suspense.'
'What would be the shortest short story you can imagine?'
'There was a nun, she got pregnant, God knows by whom.'

Thank you for your patient listening.

October 27, 2013

16. MYSTIC POETRY

Nearly twenty-five years ago, while developing a keen interest in mystic poetry, I came across a book titled *The Vision of Kabir.* In that book Kabir Das's mystic poetry was translated into English by mystic philosopher, Sehdev Kumar. In that scholarly book Sehdev Kumar not only provided an in-depth analysis of Kabir's vision and the essence of his philosophy, he also shared Kabir's insights into the psyche of mystic poetry at large. I had no idea that one day I would have the honour of meeting and befriending the translator and philosopher Sehdev Kumar.

Looking back now, I can say that mystic poet Kabir Das introduced me to mystic philosopher Sehdev Kumar and the philosopher introduced me to the poet and they both introduced me to the magic and mystery of mystic poetry. Such an introduction inspired me to further explore the rich heritage of mystic poetry, in the East as well as the West, and prompted my studies of different cultural and spiritual traditions. Let me share some highlights of my understanding of that magic and mystery. Mystic poetry has a unique position in the family of world literature because it focuses on:
• internal rather than external realities,
• inner rather than outer truths,
• metaphysical rather than physical journeys, and
• spiritual rather than materialistic worlds.

Mystic poets accept the ultimate challenge of describing the indescribable, giving form to the formless. They ask themselves:

How do we talk about a world
where sounds turn mute?
How do we write about a world
where words lose all their meanings?
How do we discuss a world
that transcends every logic?
How do we describe a world
that has no boundaries?
How do we conceptualize a world
that defies any form?
How do we understand a world

that is beyond words and sounds
and colours and space and time
and logic and.................?

An answer can be found in the words of Tagore,

"I dive down into the depths of the ocean of forms, hoping
to gain the perfect pearl of the formless." (Ref. 1)

Mystic poets are those enlightened beings who have personal encounters with the spiritual world and have touched the borders of known and unknown, the human and the divine, the personal and the cosmic. They share with us their intimate encounters with a world which is nameless, formless, timeless and pathless.

"No miseries befall one who does not cling
to name and form." ~ Buddha (Ref. 2)

"Sufism is truth without form." ~ Ibn-El-Jalali (Ref. 3)

"Pass from time and place to timelessness and placelessness,
to the other worlds. There is our origin."
~ Samarqandi Amini *(Ref. 3)*

"Truth is a pathless land." ~ Krishnamurti (Ref. 4)

When mystic poets express themselves in poetry they are more concerned about sharing their spiritual experiences, mystical encounters and existential truths than with the technique, form and language of their presentation. They are not trying to impress their readers with scholarship, seeking instead to help them open their inner eyes and connect with their own personal truths.

When we study mystic poetry created throughout the world over the centuries, we come across certain master symbols that have a universal value because they are created from the body of human experience.

The first master symbol we come across is water. Water is one of the most significant ingredients of human existence. It not only gives birth to life, it also sustains it. Most of the human body is made of water. When water takes the form of an ocean, it becomes deep and mysterious and only the daring ones have the courage to descend into its depths. Mystics are the ones who risk going to the bottom of the ocean of life to come back with the pearls of wisdom and tranquility.

Mystic poets see a human being, human self and human consciousness as a drop of water and the eternal truth and cosmic consciousness as an ocean. They claim that an ordinary man can see drops of water in an ocean but one needs special awareness and consciousness to see an ocean in a drop of water.

Kabir Das said,
"A drop
is merged
into the ocean
that everyone
understands;
but how
the ocean
is contained
in the drop
that, O my friend
only a rare man
can comprehend." (Ref. 5)

The second master symbol we come across in mystic poetry is fire. Mystic poets feel that travelling on the spiritual path is like jumping into the fire of love. If one is honest and sincere, fire transforms into a rose garden and the traveller embraces the ultimate truth; but if the traveller is an amateur and merely curious about the spiritual path then he can easily get burnt.

Rumi said,
"Love is that flame that
when it is kindled
burns everything away
God only remains." (Ref. 6)

Kabir Das shared,
"This seeking
O friend
is a stupendous task,
a raging fire
it is.
Jump in
if you wish
to be baked
but if you are
merely curious
this fire
would destroy you." (Ref. 5)

Playing with fire can be seen as adventurous but also dangerous. Only those who have confidence in themselves and in their love can dare to go close to it. Mystics embrace the flame in the certainty that they will be cleansed from all those impurities that hinder their spiritual journey. Fire purifies things, not only in our day-to-day lives but also our souls, in our spiritual lives.

William Blake wrote,
"Unless the eye catch fire
the God will not be seen
unless the ear catch fire
the God will not be heard
unless the tongue catch fire
the God will not be named
unless the heart catch fire
the God will not be loved
unless the mind catch fire
the God will not be known." (Ref. 5)

The third master symbol we come across in mystic poetry is light. Mystic poets claim that, after travelling in the dark alleys of one's soul and on the convoluted paths of the spiritual labyrinth, human beings reach a stage where they discover their inner light.

Kabir Das,
"I shall make
my body into
a clay-lamp,
my soul, its wick
and my blood oil
ah, the light
of this lamp
would reveal
the face
of my beloved
to me." (Ref. 5)

In this journey the traveller has to consume himself to discover light and be enlightened.

Baba Farid-ad-din Attar wrote,
"The true lover finds the light only if,
like the candle
he is his own fuel
consuming himself." (Ref. 7)

Anonymous,
"First you go toward the light
Next you are in the light
Then you are the light." (Ref. 4)

Alongside light being a guide in the darkest journeys of our inner self, it is also a synthesis of the colours of the rainbow. When different aspects of human life merge within, people become enlightened beings and their thoughts, words and actions become a source of light for others. They become torches that guide the lost souls.

After discovering the inner truth and light, mystics tend to speak less and avoid arguments. They prefer to remain quiet. They realize that their genuine silence can communicate more than idle talk or meaningless debates. They become aware of the limitations of words.

Madhu Lal Hussain said,

"Be never engaged at all
in arguments so long
but ponder over your end
so says Hussain Faqir." (Ref. 7)

Kabir Das wrote,
"Anyone who had a taste
of his love
is so enchanted by it
that he is stricken
with silence.
O dear friend
when you have a gem
in your hand
you don't go
on the street
announcing it." (Ref. 5)

While studying mystic poetry we are struck by the simplicity of expression. Mystic poets use simple language because they want to communicate with common people. They don't want to impress literary scholars and critics. They are humble people and their humility is reflected in their poetry. They know the art of expressing the most profound experiences in the simplest ways and are dissatisfied with those scholars and clergy who use difficult language that common people cannot understand. They feel it reflects their elitist attitude and arrogance. Mystics are critical of those pandits, maulvis, priests and rabbis who give sermons in a foreign language and offer prayers in Sanskrit, Latin, Hebrew or Arabic that the masses do not comprehend. Mystics dislike rituals and dogmas that distance people from their own truths and establish the authority of religious institutions. They encourage people to communicate and pray in their mother tongues or meditate in silence. Many mystics feel that knowledge, rather than helping to find enlightenment, can often become a hindrance in one's spiritual growth. Aldous Huxley confessed to Krishnamurti that, "He would give everything for one direct perception of the truth, but his mind was incapable of it. It was too filled with knowledge." *(Ref. 8)*

When we study Kabir's poetry we find that, being a weaver by profession he, like many other mystic poets, identified with working class people so much that his poetry is full of symbols and metaphors derived from the crafts—weaving, pottery, farming and other working class professions. He also weaves his verses with phenomena of nature so that common people can relate to his poetry.

When we study the life stories of mystic poets we become aware that many of them led simple lives. Because of their aptitude and personalities they did not fit into the formal education systems and traditional institutions of their times. They were students of the university of life and learnt from their own experiences. They followed the trails of their own hearts and souls rather than the highways of tradition and convention. One such example is Walt Whitman, a mystic poet of nineteenth-century America who has influenced twentieth-century American literature more than any other poet. Although his poems from his collection, *Leaves of Grass* are taught in colleges and universities all over the world, he himself did not do well in school. His teacher, Mr. Benjamin Halleck, was so disappointed in him that he told his father, "This boy is so idle, I am sure he will never amount to anything."

Whitman's father, agreeing with the teacher, took him out of school at age thirteen and asked him to work in a printer's shop. Even at work, he was so preoccupied with his soul-searching that his employer thought he was devoting himself to "the fine art of doing nothing."*(Ref. 9)* People failed to realize that Walt Whitman was trying to contemplate and meditate upon the mysteries of life from a very early age.

Mystic poets and their poetry have long been a mystery and a source of controversy for traditional literary critics. When we study reviews of mystic poetry, on one hand we find those who evaluate such poetry as lacking in form, style and literary beauty, while others consider it a different genre by its very nature, insisting that saints, sufis and mystics are more visionaries than poets.

Sehdev Kumar, a research scholar of the poetry of Kabir Das wrote, "…Kabir was first and foremost a visionary, his poetry is a mere 'by-product of his vision'… Kabir is a *nirgunibhakta*—a lover of the formless and infinite," and as such it should not be judged as poetry. The verses of the saints are of an entirely different genre than those of the poets. From the pen of William Kingland, we read:

"The mystic may not always be a master of language, but it is truth which he endeavours to express that we should do well to seize; and learn also to make proper allowance for the inadequacy of language to express the deepest truths. No one knows better than the greatest master of technique how inadequate are the materials with which he has to work, no one realizes more clearly than the greatest master of language, how little language can express of the living truth with which his innermost nature is on fire."
(Ref. 5)

Rumi said,
"You see through each cloak I wear
know if I speak without mouth or language
the world is drunk on its desire for words
I am the slave of the Master of silence." (Ref. 6)

July 2014

References
1. Tagore, Rabindranath. *Gitanjali*, MacMillan Publishers Ltd., London, England, 1913.
2. Buddha. *Dhammapada*, Translation by Thomas Cleary, Bantam Books, New York, 1995.
3. Shah, Idries. *The Way of the Sufi*, Penguin Books, England, 1968.
4. White, John, Editor. *What Is Enlightenment?*, Jeremy Tarcher Inc., Los Angeles, 1984.
5. Kumar, Sehdev. *The Vision of Kabir*, Alpha and Omega Books, Ontario,
Canada, 1984.
6. Harvey, Andrew. *Love's Fire - Re-creations of Rumi*, Meeramma Publications,
New York, 1988.
7. Rehman, Tariq, Editor. *Mystic Poets of Pakistan*, Pakistan

Academy of
Letters, Islamabad, 1993.
8. Jayakar, Pupul. *Krishnamurti - A Biography*, Harper and Row Publishers,
New York, 1986.
9. Thomas, Henry and Thomas, Dana Lees. *Living Biographies of Great Poets*,
Garden City Books, New York, 1984

17.   RAISING SOCIAL AND POLITICAL CONSCIOUSNESS
REFLECTIONS OF A PROGRESSIVE HUMANIST WRITER
presented at a FAMILY OF THE HEART seminar

Ladies and Gentlemen,

I feel very honoured that my creative friends Syed Azeem and Ameer Jaffri have organized this wonderful seminar. Over the decades I have published many books but I was always reluctant to agree to a book launch as it can be an embarrassing situation to sit on the stage while other people say wonderful things about you that might be more a reflection of their love than one's creativity. But this time it is different. These two books that we are launching today, *Samaji Tabdeeli, Irteqa ya inqilab* and *Al-qaeda, Amreeka aur Pakistan,* are a group effort. I am very fortunate to have a creative circle of friends that help me in my creative adventures. The dream of publishing these two books would not have come true if I did not have the support of Syed Azeem, Ameer Jaffri, Rafiq Sultan, Zahra Naqvi, Shabab Haider, Zafar Malik, Najeeb Qazmi, Darakhshanda Shehnaz, Nauroz Arif and Nighat Wein and our publisher Abbas Shad. Native Indian Black Elk once said, *"No great work can be done by one person alone."* I feel honoured that all these people gave me their trust to become part of my creative projects.

I also want to thank Gohar Taj, Baland Iqbal, Hamid Bashani, Noman Ali and Omar Latif for their scholarly reviews of my books. They are a source of inspiration for me to create better.

Why did we publish these two books? The answer, in one sentence, is *to raise social and political consciousness.*

Today I will share with you some of my reflections as a progressive humanist writer. There are many writers amongst us, and all of us have our unique ideas and ideals, ambitions and dreams. As a writer, I like to share my truth and I hope that my words inspire others to get in touch with their truth and to feel comfortable sharing it with others. As a humanist writer, I think that human beings are more important than organized religions and deities. I am against religious fundamentalism and violence associated with it. As a progressive writer, I am against Western imperialism that has been exploiting many poor and developing countries and keeping a big gap between the haves and have-nots in the world.

I support all those who want to create a just and peaceful world. My writings are my humble contributions towards that goal and dream. That is why I call my creations my love letters to humanity.

After I published my book, *From Islam to Secular Humanism...A Philosophical Journey,* I engaged in many television and radio interviews and social dialogues in living rooms. Those discussions and dialogues, even debates, were an attempt to raise social and political consciousness so we can discuss the dynamics of contemporary world politics and see what role we can play as progressive and humanist writers from the East as well as the West.

To understand the dynamics of social and political change I studied the biographies of reformers and revolutionaries of the twentieth century and wrote a book, *Prophets of Violence, Prophets of Peace.* Some of those essays were later translated into Urdu. I consider it my social responsibility, as a Pakistani and as an Urdu writer, to translate world literature into Urdu so that our people become aware of the difficulties faced by people all over the world. Some of their struggles are similar to ours and we can learn from each other. In the global village, the struggle of one nation can inspire the struggles of other nations. Such inspiration takes place through visual and print media and writers and journalists play a significant role in that process.

During my study of biographies and political movements, I became aware of two significant traditions in the twentieth century.

The first concerned reformers who wanted to bring about social change through peaceful means. They did not believe in armed struggle., believing the process of change was as important as the goals. This tradition included reformers like Leo Tolstoy, Mohandas Gandhi, Dalai Lama and Martin Luther King Jr., who inspired each other. Gandhi was inspired by Tolstoy and named his farm in South Africa Tolstoy farm, and the Dalai Lama and King were inspired by Gandhi and his philosophy of *Satyagraha.*

The second tradition concerned those revolutionaries who believed in armed struggle and claimed that the end justified the means. They were willing to take up arms against oppressive autocratic political systems and replace them with socialist systems in which the people held the power. This tradition of revolutionaries included Vladimir Lenin, Ho Chi Minh, Fidel Castro, Che Guevara, Nelson Mandela and many others. Studying these revolutionary movements, I discovered they produced two kinds of political results in the twentieth century:

a) The first group created communist states like Cuba where the Batista Government, supported by America, was overthrown and replaced by the Communist party led by Fidel Castro and Che Guevara. Later on Che tried to export that revolution to other Latin American and African countries but became a victim of CIA and Bolivian Government agents. He was killed alongside his comrades. I went to Cuba to visit Che's museum in the small town of Santa Clara where Che made his final attack on the Batista Government the day before the revolution succeeded.

b) The second group created a socialist and democratic South Africa in which Blacks said goodbye to the minority White government and, after multi-party elections, created a Black majority government. I went to South Africa to see the effects of apartheid. When I came back I wrote a book, *Kalay Jismon ki Riazat,* with the help of Jawaid Danish, to introduce Urdu writers to the struggles of Blacks in South Africa.

In the twentieth century, Nelson Mandela and his party the African National Congress (ANC), became a role-model for many other revolutionaries. Mandela had the political wisdom to negotiate not only with De Klerk, the leader of Whites, but also with Butulizi, the leader of other Black tribes. Mandela stated categorically that he did not want South Africa to be divided into eight Bantustans as he did not want to see South Africa suffer as India had when it was divided into Pakistan and Hindustan in 1947 and faced the turmoil of unresolved social, economic and political problems that persisted over decades.

In the twenty-first century, where on one hand we have the dark forces of religious fundamentalism and on the other the equally dark force of Western imperialism, we need to raise social and political consciousness so that more people become enlightened. Once enlightened, people are no longer victimized as they choose not to cooperate with their oppressors. What I learned as a psychotherapist, Ho Chi Minh was also aware of as a political activist: that people cannot be exploited, manipulated and abused for a long time against their wishes. When people become aware of their rights and are willing to fight for them, sooner or later they win the battle. Political change is slow but the rapid changes in the Middle East are making global change faster.

I am of the opinion that in the twenty-first century humanity is at a cross-roads. We can commit collective suicide with nuclear weapons and civil war, or create a just and peaceful world by joining progressive forces. People of poor countries have one thing in common. They are all suffering. The time has come for that suffering to end. But for that to happen we need leaders and followers and movements that share progressive goals. If writers play their role responsibly and political activists play their role effectively they can gain the confidence and trust of the masses and lead them. We need leaders with political integrity and political wisdom who can lead humanity to a peaceful destination. Rather than complaining about the long night of darkness I am trying to light a candle of hope and justice and peace, and I feel honoured you have joined me in lighting that candle.

We are all aware that the process of making history is slow. We need to keep the hope alive through the dark night of oppression if we are to see the dawn of freedom and justice and peace. We need to become like that old Indian grandfather who was planting a mango tree so that his grandchildren could enjoy the fruits of his hard work. Our efforts are not only for our generation but also for our children and grandchildren so that they can one day live in a peaceful world free of nuclear weapons and civil wars, a world where food, shelter, healthcare and education are universal, where no child goes to bed hungry and they are free to become the best human being they can be and take humanity to new heights. You might think I am dreamer but we need to dream in the first place if our dreams are to come true.

Since the tragedy of September 11, 2001, Pakistan has faced a serious political crisis. So many innocent Pakistani men, women and children are dying because of Muslim suicide bombers on one side and drone attacks from NATO on the other. Our books

offer an analysis of the contemporary political situation. We hope that such analysis will help Pakistanis in Pakistan, as well as in Canada, to decide what role they are going to play in the next decade. Are they going to support fundamentalists or imperialists? I, as a progressive humanist writer, support neither as I dream of a just and a peaceful world.
Thank you.

PART FOUR

Philosophical Essays

18.   HUMAN PSYCHE...SOUL OR MIND?

Historically, the human psyche was believed to be a soul. This concept was predominantly popular in Christian, Jewish and Muslim communities who deemed the soul capable of existing independently of the body. It entered a human fetus at a certain stage of development, stayed in the body throughout life and left at the time of death to return to the world of souls, so that it could be judged on the Day of Judgment and enter hell or heaven depending on its good and bad deeds.

Alongside this Judeo-Christian-Islamic belief in soul, there were Hindus and Buddhists, who followed the tradition of reincarnation and believed that the human soul returned to earth again and again to purify itself and acquire a higher or lower level of existence depending upon its good and bad deeds—the karma of the previous incarnation. This cycle of existence and suffering continued until the soul acquired enlightenment and found nirvana, thus transcending the cycle of suffering and joining the Ultimate Soul, God. There, the soul found eternal life and no longer returned to earth for any more suffering.

These models, both religious and spiritual, express a desire, a wish, a hope, for humans to enjoy eternal life and live forever. Since the human body was mortal, people believed in an immortal soul and connected that belief with the belief of their immortal and eternal God.

In the last few centuries a third model has gained popularity—the secular model. Followers of this model refer to the psyche as the mind, not the soul. The mind is intimately connected with the body and does not exist independently of it. Instead, it is an extension of the body related to the functioning of the brain and is connected with human personality, which in turn is considered responsible for choices of human lifestyle.

This secular model, in which the human psyche is understood to mean the human mind, has developed because of the advances of
...biologists like Charles Darwin
...psychologists like Sigmund Freud
...sociologists like Karl Marx
and
...existentialist philosophers like Jean Paul Sartre.

Since secular people do not believe in life after death,

they try to make their lives more meaningful and create a paradise on earth. Based on these secular models, contemporary mental health disciplines of psychiatry, psychology, nursing and social work have adopted what we call a bio-psycho-social model. According to this model, mental illness and emotional problems can be diagnosed and treated based on biological, psychological and social understanding of the patient's problems.

People suffering from schizophrenia and manic depressive illness might have a strong biological component, having genetically inherited their illness through their family. For these patients, biochemical abnormalities may exist at birth that make them vulnerable to psychological and social stresses later on. People with neurotic and personality disorders might have experienced emotional abuse or trauma as children growing up in dysfunctional and unhealthy families. Similarly immigrants might have emotional and social problems because of difficulty adjusting to a new culture and not being able to resolve social and cultural conflicts. Secular mental health professionals attempt to identify contributory factors to a person's emotional condition and suggest a combination of
Medication for biochemical disorders
Psychotherapy for psychological problems
and
Family and group therapy to resolve social conflicts.
This approach has been very effective in helping people suffering from mental illnesses and emotional problems.
In the last few decades, there has been an ongoing dialogue between professionals and lay people, mental health workers and patients about the similarities and differences in their belief systems. Different professionals have adopted different attitudes. I know some psychiatrists and nurses who refuse to discuss their religious, spiritual and secular beliefs with patients as they feel it is not important for their treatment plan. In my clinical practice if my patients ask my views directly I share with them that I am a secular humanist who respects people from all religious, spiritual and secular traditions and supports people in seeking their own truth. I believe that there are as many truths as human beings and as many realities as pairs of eyes in this world. Most of my patients are believers but we sustain mutually respectful relationships with each other. I share with them that

my role is not to enter into academic discussion about their ideology or philosophy. I am there to help them reduce their emotional suffering—whether depression, anxiety, paranoia or marital problems—and thus improve their quality of life.

While there are some atheist psychiatrists who discourage their patients from attending church and synagogue, mosque and temple gatherings, I never object to it as I believe that their attending religious and spiritual services offers them emotional and moral support as long as their religious relatives and friends do not object to the psychiatric treatment they are receiving.

I remember when my aunt in Pakistan suffered from schizophrenia. She was seen by a psychiatrist and prescribed Modecate by injection and supportive therapy. My uncle, who was a religious man, asked my opinion about taking her to see a spiritual healer because she had a lot of faith in him. I told my uncle that I did not object her seeing the spiritual healer if that is what they wished, as long as she took her Modecate injection and followed her psychiatric care plan regularly. When my aunt regained her emotional stability my uncle believed it was the result of spiritual healing, while I, as a psychiatrist, felt strongly that it was the result of the Modecate injections. Interestingly, a time came when Modecate injections became unavailable in Pakistan. My aunt started to regress and, although she was still going to see her spiritual healer, began displaying psychotic symptoms and inappropriate behaviour. My aunt's illness became a great concern for the whole family. On my uncle's request I sent Modecate injections from Canada and when my aunt started taking the injections regularly she started to improve. After that experience my aunt and uncle agreed with me that the psychiatric treatment was the cake and the spiritual practices the icing.

If we see the contemporary world we see all the religious, spiritual and secular practices existing side by side.
Some people believe in a soul and the Day of Judgment
Some people believe in a soul and re-incarnation
And
Some believe in a mind that exists as an extension of body and brain that dies when the person dies. They do not believe in life after death and the Day of Judgment.
Being a secular humanist and psychotherapist, I belong to the

third group but I have no hesitation in serving people from the first two groups. That is my way of serving humanity and people from all walks of life because as a physician I want to help people reduce their suffering and discover a healthy, happy and peaceful lifestyle. I am a psychotherapist, not a priest, and more concerned about caring for their minds than saving their souls.

19.   SCIENCE AND SPIRITUALITY
ENCOUNTERS WITH HERBERT BENSON AND DALAI LAMA

While I was reading *Freedom in Exile, the autobiography of the Dalai Lama,* I was surprised to find out that the fourteenth Dalai Lama had met with a well-respected scientist, Dr. Herbert Benson, in America and agreed for a team of Western scientists to travel to the monasteries of the Buddhist monks and record the bodily changes that took place while they were absorbed in their spiritual meditation. By the time Herbert Benson met the Dalai Lama, he had already established himself as a Behaviourist and had made valuable contributions to that field of human psychology, especially the Relaxation Response, a useful therapeutic technique for people who suffered with different kinds of tensions, anxieties, physical and emotional problems. The encounters between the Dalai Lama, the spiritual leader of the Buddhist tradition of the East, and Herbert Benson, a leader in his field of Western scientific thinking, were an attempt to build a bridge between science and spirituality. Being a student of human psychology and a practicing psychotherapist I was interested in those encounters.

As I read more about these meetings, I grew curious. Why did the Dalai Lama let a group of secular scientists meet mystics, followers of his spiritual tradition? I was also curious to learn what Herbert Benson brought back from the spiritual world of the East to the scientific world of the West after those experiments.

The Dalai Lama, in his autobiography, gives the impression of a liberal and enlightened spiritual leader willing to embrace modern science and build bridges between science and spirituality. He did confess however, that his fellow Buddhists warned him against embarking upon such a project. They did not want him to divulge sacred spiritual secrets to the leaders of a secular and atheist tradition of science that did not believe in God, religion and spirituality and followed the road of rationality, logic and objectivity. Those Buddhists were worried that Western scientists might not respect their sacred practices. He wrote,

"I knew that many Tibetans were uneasy about the idea. They felt that the practices in question should be kept confidential because they derived from secret doctrines (Ref 1 p 210)."

The Dalai Lama did not listen to his fellow Buddhists. He perceived Herbert Benson's proposal as an opportunity for Westerners to be influenced by the East. He believed that if the West was willing to offer science to the East, then the East could also offer spirituality to the West. At face value, the Dalai Lama's intentions seemed respectful and honourable. He wrote that be believed that "results of such an investigation might benefit not only science but also religious practitioners and could therefore be of some general benefit to mankind (Ref 1 p 210)."

Contemplating the Dalai Lama's autobiography, I wondered whether he also had a political motive. I thought that as a political leader with the goal of liberating Tibet from Chinese occupation, he might have wanted to please American people and their Government so that they might support him in fulfilling his political dream. I wondered whether letting American scientists enter his Buddhist monasteries was a way to win the hearts of Americans while, at the same time, teaching them a few techniques and skills to relax in their fast-paced, anxiety provoking, capitalist and industrialized lifestyles. He was aware that since more and more Americans were losing faith in their own God and religion, they might be open to adopt Eastern practices to fill that religious and spiritual vacuum. The Dalai Lama believed that Eastern Buddhist practices of meditation might help Westerners with insecurities, doubts and anxieties achieve inner peace and a calmer lifestyle. I wondered whether, by offering Westerners a gift of spirituality, he hoped that they would be more sympathetic to his political cause of liberating Tibet from Chinese occupation.

While I mentally pursued this line of thinking I was also feeling guilty and a part of me was asking myself,

'Why are you so suspicious of the Dalai Lama?'

'Why are you not giving him the benefit of the doubt?'

'Why can't you accept that the Dalai Lama is an enlightened modern mystic who would like science and spirituality and East and West to come closer and learn from each other?'

'Why do you think he has ulterior political motives?'

As I continued my inner dialogue I realized these doubts arose from my perception of the duality of the Dalai Lama's personality. In my eyes he is not just a mystic, he is also a political leader. He is quite different from all those mystics and monks who have been meditating in their monasteries for decades oblivious to the rest of the world. Those monks have no need to prove any point to the Western world. They have no desire to demonstrate to the scientists their meditation can raise body temperature to an extent where it can dry their wet clothes. They realize their spiritual practices are to find nirvana and bliss and connect them with cosmic energy so that they can experience oneness with the universe and learn the secrets of nature. For them, their spiritual salvation is gold while lowering anxiety and rising body temperature is gold-plated. They are aware that, in spite of a superficial likeness, they are quite different in essence. They are more concerned about the temperature of the soul than the body, the peace of their spirit rather than the mind and that is why they were skeptical about having a meaningful dialogue with those Western scientists who did not believe in soul and spirit. They knew there are no thermometers or electrodes or microscopes that could record spiritual enlightenment. That is why they were reluctant to participate in such experiments. But they were also faithful followers of the Dalai Lama, so they agreed. My suspicion was that the Dalai Lama's agreement might have been more as a political rather than a spiritual leader.

Since I felt guilty having such thoughts, I did not write anything about this aspect of the Dalai Lama's life when I included him in my last book titled *Prophets of Violence and Peace…20th Century Reformers and Revolutionaries.* In that book I focused on his contributions as a spiritual leader of Buddhists and a peace-loving political leader of Tibetans. I included him in the group of Leo Tolstoy, Mohandas Gandhi and Martin Luther King Jr. who were all committed to bringing political change through peaceful means and were against armed struggle, violence and holy war. While I wrote my chapter about his life, I was secretly questioning his motivation to let Herbert Benson visit monasteries. I wondered if one day I would be able to read Herbert Benson's point of view. Being a Western scientist I thought he would be more open about his encounters with the Dalai Lama and his impressions about the joint project.

So when I found the book *Beyond the Relaxation Response* written by Herbert Benson MD, I was excited to read not only about the encounter between science and spirituality but also the dialogue between Herbert Benson and the Dalai Lama as two heavyweight leaders of very different traditions. The more I read Herbert Benson's book, the more my suspicions about the Dalai Lama's ulterior political motives rang true. Herbert Benson shared in his book that when he first proposed his idea to the Dalai Lama during his visit to America, his first response was refusal. Initially, he was thinking as a monk who was a spiritual leader of Buddhist tradition and had adopted a Buddhist lifestyle to achieve salvation and spiritual enlightenment. The Dalai Lama stated,

"It would be very difficult for these abilities to be measured. The people who practice this meditation do it for religious purposes. They must be experienced in order to feel the benefits. You *must* experience it first."

But then the Dalai Lama had second thoughts. He realized he was in America, not in India, and was talking to a Western scientist, rather than an Eastern scholar. Suddenly, he realized he was being offered a political opportunity as a political leader of Tibetans. He mentally shifted gears, put on a different hat and decided to avail himself of the opportunity, as Herbert Benson writes,

"Before I could get completely discouraged, though, he returned to English again and began to muse out loud, "Still, our culture is undergoing many changes. We have been forced out of our homeland into exile." He smiled and said, "Our 'friend' to the East [the Chinese] might be impressed with a Western explanation of what we are doing. Perhaps there is some worth in allowing this study to be done. (Ref 1 p35)"

Herbert Benson realized that the Dalai Lama's blessing was as much for political reasons as for the love of building a bridge between science and spirituality, and expressed his views in these words,

"Apparently, the Dalai Lama viewed our proposal as a way to validate his religious practices to the Chinese, who had forced the monks to flee Tibet. With his culture and religious heritage in danger of dying out, the Dalai Lama saw our proposal as a way out not only to document his faith's contributions but also perhaps even to help save it from possible extinction. (Ref 1 P35)"

It is obvious from this dialogue that the Dalai Lama agreed to the proposal as a shrewd politician and not as an innocent monk. As a political leader, he tried to kill two birds with one stone. He wanted to impress upon the Westerners the value of Eastern spiritual practices while simultaneously showing the Chinese that Buddhist monasteries needed to live longer.

I felt pleased that Herbert Benson confirmed my intuition about the political motive of the Dalai Lama.

After reading about the initial meeting I grew curious about the interactions between the group of scientists and mystics in the monasteries and the nature of the gifts of spiritual practice and Eastern wisdom the scientists brought to the West. The Dalai Lama explained in his autobiography how he perceived the nature of the Western scientists' investigations when he wrote,

> "The monks in question were practitioners of Tum-mo yoga, which is designed to demonstrate proficiency in particular Tantric disciplines. By meditating on the chakras (energy centres) and nadis (energy channels), the practitioner is able to control and prevent temporarily the activity of the grosser levels of consciousness, permitting him or her to experience the subtler levels. According to Buddhist thought, there are many levels of consciousness. The grosser pertain to ordinary perception—touch, sight, smell and so forth—whilst the subtler are those apprehended at the time of death. One of the aims of Tantra is to enable the practitioner to 'experience' death, for it is then that the most powerful spiritual realizations can come about. (Ref 1 p 210)"

It is obvious from this description that the spiritual practices of Buddhist monks are embedded in their religious faith and tradition. The Dalai Lama also described the results of Herbert Benson's experiments in these words,

> "When the grosser levels of consciousness are suppressed, physiological phenomena can be observed. In Dr. Benson's experiments, these included the raising of body temperatures (as measured internally by rectal thermometer and externally by skin thermometer) by up to 18 Fahrenheit (10 Centigrade). These increases allowed sheets, soaked in cold water and draped round them, to dry out even though the ambient temperature was well below freezing. Dr. Benson also witnessed, and took similar measurements from monks sitting naked on snow. He found they could remain still throughout

the night without any loss of body temperature. During these sessions, he also noted that the practitioner's oxygen intake decreased to around seven breaths per minute. (Ref 1 p 211)"

From the Dalai Lama's description it seems he was very proud of his monk's performance. It was as though he was describing a Hollywood performance worthy of an Oscar. Herbert Benson shared that before he started the experiments the Dalai Lama had made a request of his monks, "For skeptics, you must show something spectacular, because without that, they won't believe (Ref 2 p 45)."

The Dalai Lama knew that scientists don't believe in blind faith, only in what they can observe and record. So he wanted the monks to perform in such a way that Dr. Benson's thermometers could record the changes. On this occasion the monks performed spiritual practices not to please God but to please the Dalai Lama and impress Western scientists.

When Herbert Benson visited the monasteries he admired the simple lifestyle of those monks who had dedicated their lives to spiritual enlightenment. He introduces one of them in these words,

"The Venerable G.J., who was fifty-nine years old when we met him, had been a monk since he was thirteen. He had studied in Tibet for nineteen years and then later in India for eight years. During this period, he had earned the title *Geshe*, or doctor of philosophy, and had thereby risen to one of the highest levels of scholarship... For the past eleven years, the Venerable G.J. had lived in near-total isolation in the foothills of the Himalayas and, along with his other religious rites, had practiced *Tum-mo* Yoga for fifteen minutes each day for the last ten years. But he said he still had not achieved the 'state of bliss' that was the ultimate goal of the masters who followed this form of Yoga. (Ref 2 p 53)"

Herbert Benson described some of the results of G,J 's meditation practices in these words,

"Although his inner body temperature remained stable throughout the experiment, the temperature in G.J's fingers increased by more than 9 degrees Fahrenheit. His toe temperature rose even more strikingly – up nearly 13 degrees Fahrenheit (Ref 2 p 56)."

Herbert Benson performed similar experiments with other monks and found comparable results. From those observations he concluded that, while normal people start shivering in cold temperatures and suffer frostbite in extreme cold due to constriction of blood vessels in the extremities in an effort to conserve body heat,

> "...the Tibetan monks were saying that they were able to retard or eliminate the constriction process [of blood vessels] just by practicing certain mental and spiritual disciplines. This was an exciting idea for me for several reasons. First of all, I knew that scientific documentation of their claims would further support the existence of a strong basic relationship between the mind and the body. Also, such evidence would suggest that the *conscious* mind can play a much greater role in controlling the body's physical processes than many Western scientists had previously thought. (Ref 2 p 49)"

After Herbert Benson returned from his scientific and spiritual adventure he added a Faith Factor to his Relaxation Response and wrote *Beyond the Relaxation Response,* in which he stated, "The Relaxation Response when coupled with the power of belief can lead to remarkable health-promoting elements, which I have identified throughout as the Faith Factor (Ref 2 p vii)."

In the Faith Factor Herbert Benson tried to make a liaison between his secular scientific world of Relaxation Response and the religious world of spiritual practices.

Before going to India, Herbert Benson had established himself as a scientist and had discovered that by teaching people certain behavioural practices, they could learn a Relaxation Response that would lower tension and anxiety and help them cope with life stresses, as well as a wide range of physical illnesses. For Herbert Benson, the Faith Factor was the icing on the cake. It increased the value—the meaningfulness and usefulness—of the techniques he had already developed. As he saw it, the monks had shown him that a strong belief in one's religious tradition and a strong faith in one's spiritual values enhanced the Relaxation Response. Herbert Benson explained it's benefits for lay people in these words,

> "The term *Relaxation Response,* for those who may be unfamiliar with the concept, refers to the inborn capacity of the body to enter a special state characterized by lowered heart rate, decreased rate of breathing, lowered blood pressure,

slower brainwaves, and an overall reduction in the speed of metabolism. In addition, the changes produced by this Response counteract the harmful effects and uncomfortable feelings of stress....In this relatively peaceful condition, the individual's mental patterns change so that he breaks free of what I call "worry cycles?"

I was surprised that Herbert Benson focused his discussion ostensibly on the benefits of behavioural techniques and did not discuss its limitations. He did not mention that such practices control only the symptoms of anxiety and do not solve the underlying emotional problems addressed by practitioners of other schools of thought—whether psychoanalysts, interpersonal psychotherapists or logo-therapists—who believe that in dealing only with the symptoms of anxiety, medication or behavioural techniques are no different from taking painkillers for headaches. If the headaches are not ordinary headaches but a symptom of broncho-pneumonia then we need to offer antibiotics alongside painkillers, and if the headaches are the symptom of a brain tumour then we need to do surgery to remove the tumour in addition to offering temporary pain relief.

Those mental health professionals who, like Herbert Benson, have a behavioural approach to anxiety disorders face criticism from other schools of thought including:

...psychoanalysts who help their patients resolve and dissolve underlying emotional conflicts to relieve anxiety and tension

...interpersonal therapists who help their clients resolve their conflicts with their loved ones in order to lead a harmonious and peaceful life

...logo-therapists who help their patients discover a personal sense of meaning to help them cope with life's difficulties, and many others who believe that behaviourists like Herbert Benson are only touching the surface of the human condition. They are concerned about people who are anxious because their marriages and family relationships are failing and are going through a crisis of faith as their lives fall apart. For these people, twice daily meditation sessions might be good but not good enough. If they have a faith in God or religion they can rely on that to enhance their Relaxation Response but for many, anxiety is the product of doubt they are experiencing in their basic faith in life, in love and in the religious traditions they were brought up in.

Mystics and monks try to help people adopt a spiritual lifestyle, not just spiritual rituals twice a day or week. They perceive the Western spiritual crisis as developing through a loss of Christian faith. For many, Christianity became more of a Sunday service and divorced from the spiritual teachings of Christ. The enlightened Buddhist mystics believe that the teachings of Christ were not much different from those of Buddha so for Christians there is no need to travel thousands of miles to Buddhist monasteries and study skin temperatures and relaxation responses, they can discover that in their backyard by analyzing the dichotomy between religious practices on Sundays and secular practices during the rest of the week. The anxieties Westerners feel, both individually and collectively, lie in the dichotomy between their personal and social psyche; their solutions need to be born from the womb of their own problems. The religious and spiritual practices of a culture are like fruit trees of that land. It is not easy to transplant Indian mango trees into an Arizona desert best suited to cacti. The seeds of foreign fruits need unique soil to grow. Westerners, with their fast food psyche, feel they can import Eastern spices and spiritual practices and enjoy them. They do not realize that to develop a taste for food might be easier than seeking benefit from spiritual practices. Those practices are the outcome of a certain cultural tradition. It is no different from trying to import the Western secular psychotherapy practices to patients brought up in Eastern culture who are unfamiliar with Western values and practices. Benefiting from the spiritual practices of another tradition to achieve enlightenment is not as easy as it might seem on the surface. Eastern meditation and Western relaxation might have some parallels but the differences are more marked than the similarities.

Eastern meditation practices have evolved to achieve nirvana. Western relaxation practices are developed to help patients cope with clinical anxiety. Both are valid in their own right and fruitful for the needs of their people. But we need to realize that Western Clinical Psychology is designed to help patients cope with emotional problems and mental illness, while Eastern spiritual practices are ways to develop spiritual enlightenment. Eric Fromm highlighted that difference in his comparison of psychoanalysis and Zen Buddhism in these words.

"But in spite of the fact that both psychoanalysis and Zen deal with the nature of man and with a practice leading to his transformation, the differences seem to outweigh the similarities. Psychoanalysis is a scientific method, nonreligious to its core. Zen is a theory and technique to achieve 'enlightenment', an experience which, in the West, would be called religious or mystical. Psychoanalysis is a therapy for mental illness; Zen is a way of spiritual salvation. (Ref 2 p 123)"

It is unfortunate that many lay people, as well as mental health professionals, in the West are unaware of these differences and confuse treatments of emotional problems with methods to achieve spiritual salvation. The differences are not only between Zen and psychoanalysis, they can be seen in different professional, religious, spiritual and cultural traditions of East as well as the West. Encounters between the Dalai Lama and Herbert Benson were not only encounters between two leaders of science and spirituality but also between two cultures.

Being an Eastern psychiatrist who practices psychotherapy in the West, I am quite aware of those differences as I see them in my clinical practice. Those differences become thorny issues in dealing with Eastern immigrants living in the West as they have a different worldview. To build a bridge between Eastern patients and Western psychiatric practices is not easy. John Triselistis, a trans-cultural psychiatrist highlights this dilemma in these words,

"Psychiatry being mainly the product of Western religious beliefs, of a capitalistic economic system and of individualistic ideologies, is largely alien to cultures which have not gone through the same process. Western culture, by focusing almost wholly on the individual, places unusual importance on such concepts as self-alliance, self help, privacy, individual identity and independence. It is not surprising, therefore, that white mental health professionals are more sensitive to the dangers of fostering client dependency than to failure to respond to needs.

In contrast many of the attitudes and much of the behaviour of minorities have originated from cultural backgrounds which put emphasis on group and family relationships. These in turn tend to foster greater interdependence. Behaviour fashioned by such influences imposes a different approach to living, the making of relationships, the seeking of help and the resolution of problems from that found in Western societies."

It is quite obvious from this description that differences in attitudes of doctors, patients and their families are embedded in cultural traditions. Herbert Benson, being a Western scientist and a therapist, tries to help his patients as individuals. He focuses on behavioural techniques they can learn to cope with the symptoms of anxiety. But he does not acknowledge that it is just the tip of the iceberg.

Cultural and professional differences between East and West are significant and profound. For Westerners to follow Eastern practices is probably as difficult as it is for Easterners to follow Western practices. Socio-economic factors play as significant a role as religious ones. Professional and spiritual practices derived from developing countries and socialistic communities are worlds apart from those of developed countries and capitalistic communities. It is hard to adopt behaviours from other cultures without adopting the whole cultural and spiritual philosophy, as those behaviours are an integral part of that particular lifestyle. In the last few decades, trans-cultural psychiatry is trying to build those bridges but the whole process is still in its infancy.

While Herbert Benson was developing his theory of Faith Factor in Relaxation Response, he was challenged by other behaviourists and psychologists who were of the opinion that secular relaxation practices are qualitatively different from Transcendental Meditation. Herbert Benson shared one such encounter in these words,

"I was astonished to see Dr. Robert Keith Wallace, my original collaborator years before in studying the physiological impact of meditation on members of the Transcendental Meditation movement. We had not seen each other for more than six years.

Although we had started experiments independently of one another, we had come to the same conclusion: There were measurable physiological changes that resulted from meditation. For a while, we joined to collaborate our data and publish our findings, but we later disagreed over the universality of the changes that could take place with different types of meditation, and so we parted ways. In short, he felt there was something unique about the techniques of Transcendental Meditation that caused the changes. I, on the other hand, believed the key physical changes could be elicited regardless of any particular meditation technique. (Ref 2 p 41)"

It is obvious from the description that Dr. Herbert Benson and Dr. Robert Wallace had different orientations, one focused on the physical and physiological changes while the other gave the spiritual dimension the same importance as the physical and believed those experiences might look the same but are qualitatively different.

It was interesting to read how Herbert Benson tried to make his theory of Faith Factor multicultural and multi-faith. He wanted to focus on the faith dimension not realizing that each tradition has its own special dynamics. Ironically, the building he erected on the foundation of Faith Factor became shaky when he had to deal with atheists and agnostics. He suggested they could focus on any word like "One' and could get the same results. He wrote,

"...if you don't happen to affirm a traditional religious faith, the Faith Factor can still be an important, healing part of your life. In fact, the research has shown that *any* neutral sound or word can be effective in eliciting the Relaxation Response. So even if you deny that religious or broad philosophical convictions are valid at all, you can get significant benefits from the Faith Factor. Simply pick a word like 'one' which I described in my initial instructions for eliciting the Relaxation Response. (Ref 2 p 110)"

For me, if any word is as effective as God, Allah and Bhagwan then I feel the whole premise of Faith Factor crumbles. Reading that section of the book I felt as if the Faith Factor theory faced a faith crisis when facing people with no faith.

Reading Herbert Benson's book about the Relaxation Response, I was impressed by the techniques he developed for his patients to learn to relax and decrease their anxiety levels. He explains his technique in these words,

"Certain meditative and prayerful instructions can be employed to elicit the Relaxation Response. A simple technique I use to bring the Relaxation Response in people is a four-step procedure that involves:

1. finding a quiet environment
2. consciously relaxing the body muscles
3. focusing for ten to twenty minutes on a mental device, such as the word *one* or a brief prayer
4. assuming a passive attitude toward intrusive thoughts (Ref 2 p 5)"

I was not impressed by the Faith Factor as it did not seem integral to the whole process. I thought that, while studying the Buddhist monks he focused so much on the superficial aspects of meditation by recording the skin temperatures, he missed that each of the monks he studied had dedicated their lives to spiritual enlightenment. They had offered numerous sacrifices all their lives for their spiritual growth. For those monks to meditate twice a day for half an hour was quite different than for a sales-rep from California who buys a lottery ticket every week out of an ambition to be rich one day. He works aggressively every day to become the President of his company, buy a half a million dollar house with an outdoor pool for his wife, three children and a dog, a garage for his Jaguar, and a cottage in the country. After reading Herbert Benson's book he might contemplate building a quiet room in his house so he can meditate twice a day to feel relaxed and cope with his hectic job, family stresses, and social life. He does not realize that, for all his good intentions, Herbert Benson is offering him a fast food hamburger, which is different from the home-cooked meal of the East. For monks, spirituality is like wine and love, which demand a lot of patience but get better with the passage of time. Herbert Benson acknowledged the lifestyles of monks in these words, "...many monks spend several years...with almost no contact with the outside world. Pious supporters leave them their food weekly just outside their huts (Ref 2 p 52)."

For me, recommending Relaxation Response with Faith Factor is like suggesting sex as an exercise program to lose calories. Lovers might lose calories during their intimate encounters, but for them sex is making love, which is a profound emotional and mystical experience. For monks, a rise in body temperature and lowering of tension is part of the spiritual bliss they achieve in their daily religious practices. I wonder, how can any thermometer, electrode or microscope record the spiritual changes they experience? A philosopher once said. "Everything that counts cannot be counted." That is where a scientist and a mystic have a different view of life. Mystics look for experiences that count while scientists look for information that can be counted. One focuses on words, the other on meanings; one looks for the body changes, the other for the spiritual changes. Ironically, both kinds of changes can co-exist. The point is, which one of those changes is more important and desired? Eastern monks know that spiritual changes are accompanied by bodily changes, but the Western behaviourists are still unwilling to accept that the physical changes of relaxation are not necessarily accompanied by the spiritual changes.

For me one of the significant questions was, 'why did Herbert Benson feel the need and urge to meet the Dalai Lama and fly to Tibet to meet monks? If he was interested in the spiritual dimension of life he could have tested Christians, Muslims and Jews living in America and record the bodily changes while they pray. He might have found similar changes to prove his hypothesis of the mind's power over the body, especially during spiritual practice. I wondered if it was the exotic part of Buddhist tradition and spiritual practice that he had absorbed through books and film that inspired him to follow that road.

He wanted to be the first Western scientist to record those experiences. He wanted to be on the cutting edge, to build a bridge between Eastern mysticism and Western science. It sounded more like a Hollywood performance. He confessed, "The Dalai Lama had obviously made it possible for us to test the monks and to measure things that *no scientist had ever done before.*" [italics are mine]

While I was reading Herbert Benson's adventures, I remembered Abraham Maslow, another well-respected psychologist of the West who had a keen interest in the spiritual dimension of human life. He believed that we did not need to travel thousands of miles in pilgrimage to discover spirituality; we can easily find it in our own backyards. He wrote,

"The search for the exotic, the strange, the unusual, the uncommon, has often taken the form of pilgrimages, of turning away from the world, the 'journey of the East' to another country or to a different religion. The great lesson from the true mystics, from the Zen monks, and now also from the Humanistic and Transpersonal psychologists…that the sacred is in the ordinary, that is to be found in one's daily life, in one's neighbours, friends and family, in one's backyard, and that travel may be a flight from confronting the sacred…this lesson can be easily lost. To be looking elsewhere for miracles is to me a sign of ignorance that everything is miraculous. (Ref 3 p 79)"

Rather than going to the East like Herbert Benson, Maslow studied the spiritual experiences of people in the West and made valuable contributions to human psychology. Maslow's concepts of peak experiences and self-actualization are well respected even after his death.

After finishing the Dalai Lama's and Herbert Benson's books, I wondered whether both achieved their goals. The Dalai Lama still lives in exile after 40 years of leaving Tibet. He did receive a Nobel Peace prize but could not convince Americans and other Western countries to assist him in liberating Tibet. On the other hand Herbert Benson has developed a big following in the field of Behavioural Sciences. He has added the Faith Factor to his philosophy. For me, his contributions as a secular scientist who offered Relaxation Response to all those men and women who suffer from anxiety is a great contribution to humanity but his Faith Factor does not impress me.

Although Herbert Benson went all the way to Tibet to meet Buddhist monks I wondered whether he had the right attitude towards their spiritual practices. Buddhist monks were reluctant to have secular scientists examine and scrutinize their practices. Herbert Benson shared that feeling in these words,

"Before we were allowed to view the practice of *lung gom-pa* it was necessary first to be initiated. When the monks took their vows, they were told that that if they disclosed their practices to the uninitiated, both they and their viewers would go to hell forever. Accordingly, the Dalai Lama's intercession permitted us to be initiated through listening to the recital of Buddhist scriptures. (Ref 2 p 157) "

Herbert Benson listened to the scriptures but did not develop any reverence for their spiritual teachings and practices. He persistently viewed them with skepticism. He shared his observations in these words,

"Two monks, the Venerable K.G. , aged seventy, and the Venerable T.P. aged thirty-four, then demonstrated their practice. They dressed only in loincloths and sat in a cross-legged position upon a small pile of carpets. They carried out a number of physical exercises in unison, including deep breathing, slapping their hands against their own chests, arms, and legs; and swaying. As these were performed, they chanted. They stood, rapidly crossed their legs into a cross-legged position, and fell to the ground with their legs remaining crossed…The young monk stood, bent his knees slightly, and jumped three to four feet into the air, with his legs straight. While in the air, he rapidly assumed the cross-legged position and fell to the ground while maintaining this position. He landed with a resounding crash as he slapped his crossed legs outward and downward...We asked whether what we had seen was the so-called "levitation meditation" and were told that indeed it was. (Ref 2 p 157)"

It seems as if Herbert Benson, in spite of initiation, did not see those practices as spiritual and holy and sacred, otherwise he would not have written,

"We had witnessed a remarkable athletic performance, but there was no floating or hovering. The fact that only the younger monk could perform the exercise also suggested it was athletic, not spiritual. If spiritual, one would have suspected the older monk would be more proficient. (Ref 2 p 158)"

While I was reading that assessment of Herbert Benson, comparing spiritual practices to athletic acrobats, it reminded me of the directions the Dalai Lama had given to his monks, "For skeptics, you must show something spectacular, because without that, they won't believe (Ref 2 p 45)."

Unfortunately, in spite of the spectacular performances the skeptics were not convinced they were spiritual. It was ironic to read that Herbert Benson, in spite of adding Faith Factor to his Relaxation Response did not have faith in the spiritual practices of Buddhist monks. He seems to have added Faith Factor more from a pragmatic point of view as a scientist rather than as someone who believed in the sacredness of spiritual practices. For him, meditation was more of an exercise to calm one's nerves rather than a profound encounter with the cosmos. He did not appreciate that monks had dedicated their lives and had been involved in those spiritual practices to find bliss. More preoccupied with the physiological than the spiritual he wrote,

"Whatever theological or philosophical reasons be given for the power of meditation in these cultures, the techniques all commonly elicit what we today call the Relaxation Response (Ref 2 p 101)."

It seems to me that,what Eastern mystics consider the most important aspect of meditation, the Western scientists consider the least important part. For mystics the spiritual enlightenment is the goal while for the scientists the Relaxation Response is the aim. They might meet at the same airport but are planning to travel in different directions.

Reading Herbert Benson's book I am not convinced he, as a scientist, is able to differentiate between the Relaxation Response that is useful for anxious patients to cope with daily stress and the meditation that is the pathway to spiritual enlightenment. From initiating Relaxation Response, to maintaining Relaxation Response, to a lifestyle of peace and harmony, people need to journey far along a road less traveled. For Herbert Benson, a Western scientist, to appreciate the mysteries of Eastern mysticism is not easy. He took the first step but it seems he could not travel further. In the beginning of the book he seems aware of the journey he was undertaking. He wrote,

"My function in exploring and describing this faith Factor is to serve, as best as I can, as a bridge between two disciplines: traditional faith and meditative practices and scientific observation...I realize in stating this purpose that I'm embarking along a fine line that separates two conflicting ways of thinking---and that this combination may be potentially problematic. (Ref 2 p 6)"

By the end of the book he is swayed by the pragmatic scientist in him who wants to help his patients suffering from physical and emotional problems and ignores the spiritual dimension of meditation. His publisher promotes Herbert Benson's work in these words,

"A practical program that may help you

...relieve headaches, backaches, chest pains

...lower blood pressure and cholesterol

...eliminate insomnia and decrease anxiety.

In just minutes a day you can easily master the STRESS REDUCTION techniques that have helped millions conquer or alleviate one of today's most serious and widespread health problems."

While I was reading this commercial about Herbert Benson's miraculous Relaxation Response and Faith Factor techniques, I remembered why the Dalai Lama was warned by other Buddhist monks not to invite a Western scientist to the East. He had stated, "I knew that many Tibetans were uneasy about the idea. They felt that the practices in question should be kept confidential because they derived from secret doctrines." They were afraid that a Western scientist living in the capitalist world might start selling spirituality like burgers in a fast food restaurant, giving the impression that spiritual practices could be learnt and adopted in weekend seminars.

It seems the encounter between the Dalai Lama and Herbert Benson was a brief moment in time when East and West fleetingly touched each other. For one, the experience was physical, for the other, metaphysical; for one it was secular, for the other sacred; for one it seemed athletic for the other spiritual. Existentially speaking, two people sharing the same experience can have two different, sometimes opposite, interpretations and meanings. Encounters between spirituality and science, mystic East and materialistic West are still in infancy. Both cultures still need to do some soul-searching before they can develop a cooperative and harmonious relationship rather than a confrontational and conflicted one, learn from each other and discover universal humanistic values and lifestyles.

References

1.   Lama Dalai...Freedom in Exile
      Harper Perennial Publishers Canada 2000

2.   Benson Herbert MD ...Beyond the Relaxation Response
      Berkley Books New York USA 1984

3.   Sohail K Dr. ...From Islam to Secular Humanism
      Abbeyfield Publishers Canada 2001

20   SECULAR SPIRITUALITY

I just finished reading Dr Jill Taylor's book, *My Stroke of Insight* (Ref. 1), a wonderful, awesome and inspiring book that tells the story of a brain expert who experiences a brain injury. More specifically, it is the journey of a neuroscientist who experiences a stroke and loses the faculties of the left side of her brain due to hemorrhage. The mental functions she lost within hours took her years to regain. The story takes us from a breakdown to a breakthrough.

Being a psychiatrist and a practicing psychotherapist, I am curious about the functions of the brain and fascinated with the mysteries of the mind. One of the things I found amazing about Jill's journey was that, although she lost the functions of her left brain and could not walk, talk, think logically and use words, she still retained the functions of her right brain. Thus, her story provides wonderful insights into the right brain functions, the part of the brain that deals with the mysteries of creativity as well as spirituality.

I have read descriptions of spiritual experiences in religious and holy books but this is the first time I have encountered a biological, neurological and secular description of spirituality. It is a description that can be accepted by a priest as well an atheist as it is based on human experience rather than belief and blind faith. Jill describes what she saw, felt and experienced. A scientist, she describes her illogical or supra-logical experiences in a logical way and provides profound secular insights into spirituality. She highlights how the experiences of the right brain, that transcend traditional rationality, cannot be satisfactorily described by the logic and language of the left brain.

Jill Taylor, being a teacher, describes the left brain ability to register the spatial dimensions of the human body and recognize the separateness of the person from the environment. When that sense is lost the person with a functioning right brain feels at one with the universe. It is like a drop feeling part of the ocean—some call it an oceanic feeling. It is a wonderful and peaceful experience. She writes,

"By the end of that morning, my consciousness shifted into a perception that I was at *one* with the universe. Since that time, I have come to understand how it is that we are capable of having a 'mystical' or 'metaphysical' experience—relative to our brain anatomy…(Ref 1. p 3)"

"Ultimately, it's about my brain's journey into my right hemisphere's consciousness, where I became enveloped in a deep inner peace…As my consciousness slipped into a state of peaceful grace, I felt ethereal (Ref 1. p 43)."

Losing function in the left brain also changes the experience of time. Left brain divides time into past, present and future; into yesterday, today and tomorrow and yesteryear, this year and next year. A person with only right brain function experiences every moment and lives in the *now* without relating it to the flow of time. She writes,

"To the right mind, no time exists other than the present moment, and each moment is vibrant with emotion…To our right mind, the moment of NOW is timeless and abundant (Ref1. p 30)."

"And here, deep within the absence of earthly temporality, the boundaries of my earthly body dissolved and I melted into the universe…I'm no authority, but I think the Buddhists would say I entered the mode of existence they call Nirvana (Ref1. p 49)."

Although Jill Taylor experienced that peace, she was also completely dependent on her doctors, nurses and her mother to look after her for years. Because of the dysfunction of her left brain she had lost the balance of the right and left brain and was incapable of leading an independent life.

In losing functioning of the left brain people also lose some of their social and cultural conditioning and the sense of judgment associated with it. The left brain controls judgement of ourselves and others, sometimes quite harshly. Without the left-brain influence, the right brain freely accepts the self and others unconditionally, paving the way for unconditional love. The right brain person feels good, wonderful and awesome and considers oneself beautiful. Jill writes, "I perceived myself as perfect, whole, and beautiful just the way I was (Ref1, p 71)."

Jill Taylor brings to our attention that people who remain in touch with their right brain are:
…more peaceful
…more accepting of themselves and others
…less judgmental

...live in the moment

and

...feel a part of the universe.
These characteristics have been described in many holy books hundreds of years ago. The Bhagawad Gita states,

> *"Meditation helps humans to find peace of mind*
> *It helps people to transcend the rewards of their actions*
> *Such people do not hate anyone.*
> *They are even kind to animals.*
> *They are no longer arrogant and conceited and egotistical.*
> *They can control their anger and become forgiving.*
> *They are no longer anxious and sad and worried.*
> *They can rise above their worldly desires and become caring and compassionate"*

....

Be friendly and compassionate
Released from ego selfishness
Patient, hate not any being
The same in pain and happiness   *(Ref 3. p 83)*

....

Described are the characteristics of those people in touch with their right brain who lead peaceful and loving lives. These are the characteristics saints and sufis, monks and mystics seek to develop through meditation and other spiritual practices. Many followers of spiritual traditions—whether Muslim, Christian, Jewish or Hindu—not only acquire spiritual enlightenment themselves like Buddha, but also seek to inspire others. One such twentieth century mystic, admired by Easterners as well as Westerners, was Jiddu Krishnamurti. Raised under the tutelage of Charles Webster Leadbeater and Annie Besant of the Theosophic Society of India, who believed he had spiritual potential, he was brought to England for his spiritual grooming.

In 1922, Krishnamurti was first invited to Sydney, Australia for a Theosophical convention, where he met his old teacher Leadbeater, and later on flew to Ojai, California, which was the beginning of a new chapter of his life. His mystical experiences, gained through regular meditation, formed the beginning of his spiritual enlightenment. Some experiences were very painful, traumatic and bizarre. Most people around Krishnamurti were unable to fully understand those experiences but were supportive of his mysterious mystical journey. They believed that he was experiencing the awakening of his spiritual self, generally known in the spiritual world as *kundalini* in which the person experiences transformation of consciousness not accessible to ordinary people. One such experience Krishnamurti described to Mrs Besant in a letter,

"The climax was reached on the 19th. I could not think, nor was I able to do anything, and I was forced by friends here to retire to bed. Then I became almost unconscious, though I was well aware of what was happening around me. I came to myself at about noon each day. On that first day while I was in that state and more conscious of the things around me, I had the first most extra-ordinary experience. There was a man mending the road; that man was myself, the pickaxe he held was myself; the very stone which he was breaking was a part of me; the tender blade of grass was my very being and the tree beside the man was myself. I almost could feel and think like the road-mender, and I could feel the wind passing through the tree and the little ant on the grass I could feel. The birds, the dust and the very noise were a part of me. Just then there was a car passing by at some distance; I was the driver, the engine and the tires; as the car went further away from me, I was going away from myself. I was in everything; or rather everything was in me, inanimate and animate, the mountain, the worm and all breathing things. All day long I remained in this happy condition...I have seen the glorious and healing Light...I am God-intoxicated. (Ref 2)"

This experience is similar to what Jill Taylor shared as being 'one with the universe' after her stroke.

For the next few months, Krishnamurti continued to have these mystical experiences and spiritual encounters. During a number of those episodes he became semi-conscious and his brother and friends had to look after him to ensure he did not hurt himself. Many times he would fall to the floor in a trance and experience seizure-like states. In 1929, he said, "*The vision is total. To me that is liberation*" After that liberation, he resigned from the Theosophical Society and started his solitary journey as a mystic. He stated his philosophy in these words,

"I maintain that Truth is a pathless land, and you cannot approach it by any path whatsoever, by any religion, by any sect...Truth being limitless, unconditioned, unapproachable by any path whatsoever, cannot be organized; nor should any organization be formed to lead or to coerce people along any particular path (Ref 2)."

After resigning from the Theosophical Society, for the next half-century, Krishnamurti traveled around the world giving lectures, meeting people from all walks of life and sharing his knowledge, experience and wisdom. He inspired thousands of people to rise above religious institutions and follow the wisdom of their own hearts. Those who consulted him were not only lay people but three generations of Indian prime ministers: Jawarlal Nehru, his daughter Indira Gandhi and her son Rajev Gandhi. The Dalai Lama, George Bernard Shaw, Aldous Huxley, Henry Miller, R D Laing, Joseph Campbell and many more admired his knowledge and wisdom. He was one of the most respected mystics of twentieth century.

In many cases it takes saints years of commitment and contemplation to develop mystic personalities as loving and peaceful people. Jill Taylor developed those features because of a neurological tragedy, a stroke. Her stroke became a mixed blessing as it transformed her into a spiritual person. As she recovered, she had to choose to regain some of the functions of the left brain to function effectively in this world but decided not to develop those features that did not help her in leading a peaceful life. Recovering from her debilitating stroke, she became wiser and developed a rare insight into life. No wonder she called her book, *My Stroke of Insight.*

I feel optimistic that Jill Taylor's book can develop a bridge between religious, spiritual and secular people so that they can develop insights into those practices and experiences that are traditionally discussed in religious and holy books and develop a language that can be used to share our experiences and insights. Developing a language and discipline of secular spirituality will help people all over the world learn from the wisdom of all traditions. It is the road of the twenty-first century and our collective future. It will help us rise above the culture of war, violence and judgment and pave the way for love, acceptance and peace in the world. I would like to congratulate Jill Taylor for sharing her story and profound insights. She will be an inspiration for men and women all over the world.

References

1. Taylor Jill. *My Stroke of Insight,*
   Viking Publishers New York USA 2006

2. Jayakar Papal *Krishnamurti…A Biography*
   Harper and Rowe Publishers New York 1985

3. Parrinder Geoffrey *The Bhagavad Gita…A Verse Translation*
   One World Publishers USA 1996

21.   *GOD IS A METAPHOR*

Being a secular humanist I do not believe in any God or organized religion, but as a poet I am fascinated by all the languages and metaphors human beings have created over the centuries to understand and explain the mysteries of life and nature. Rather than saying God created human beings, it might be more appropriate to say that human beings created the image of God, and that God's image appears as a metaphor in different mythologies all over the world. The God metaphor is like a Rorschach test, where each culture has given it different names, for example, Allah, Bhagwan, or Khuda, and has projected onto it a number of human qualities. When different religious mythologies say,

God is light

God is love

Or

God is closer to you than your jugular vein,

these statements can be interpreted as metaphors rather than concrete realities. Many religions, recognizing the tendency of human beings to concretize the deity, are opposed to the creation and veneration of physical representations of God, which they call idolatry.

Psychologists are well aware that symbolic and metaphorical thinking develops only when the human mind reaches a certain level of emotional and mental maturity. As children pass through adolescence they begin to develop abstract thinking, and by the time they reach adulthood, are able to appreciate metaphors. That is the stage at which they can appreciate world literature and enjoy the multiple meanings of poems, plays and folktales.

Psychiatrists understand that when mentally healthy adults experience a nervous breakdown and suffer from psychosis, one of the signs of regression is the loss of the capacity for abstraction—they are unable to interpret metaphors. During the psychiatric interview and mental status examination, when they are asked to interpret a proverb like, "Too many cooks spoil the broth" they say something like, "If too many people go to the kitchen they start fighting and ruin the dinner." They are unable to apply that proverb to other aspects of life— they cannot generalize it. They show concrete thinking and an inability to appreciate the metaphor.

Just as we use abstract thinking to interpret a proverb, we also need an appreciation of metaphors to enjoy poems and plays and interpret scriptures, which are part of a cultural folklore. It is unsurprising then, that when scriptures are read by more evolved minds, they are interpreted in a metaphorical way, but when the same texts are read by less evolved minds, they are interpreted very literally. Unfortunately, those literal interpretations have been a source of conflict in religious families and communities, creating wars between different sects and religions.

The belief of many Muslims that their prophet Mohammad went to seventh heaven to meet God is possible only if they conceive of God as living in a special corner of the universe. Otherwise they will believe that Mohammad had a special mystical experience that could not be explained in ordinary language and that he therefore shared metaphorically. Similarly, for Christians to believe that Christ ascended physically to heaven to be with his Holy Father, they have to understand God as an entity living somewhere in the skies. Many enlightened readers of scriptures view Mohammad's and Christ's ascending experiences as symbolic not physical, metaphorical not concrete.

If we encourage our children to study scriptures as part of folklore and wisdom literature we must help them develop their critical and creative thinking so that they can enjoy and appreciate cultural symbols and metaphors of world poetry, plays and folktales. Scriptures were written in the context of a particular pre-existing language and culture; it is only by appreciating those linguistic and cultural traditions that we can understand their scriptures as part of their mythology. Since scriptures reflect the psyche of that culture and the traditions of the era in which they were created, future generations decide their relevance to their contemporary existential and social problems.

If we pursue this line of thinking further, we can see that language itself is a metaphor and is a creative expression of that culture. Words are symbols reflecting something else. Words can be interpreted in a concrete way as part of an ordinary statement but become symbolic and metaphorical if they are part of literature. The word *mother* can be someone's mother or can represent all mothers. Similarly *mothering* can be a metaphor for caring and nurturing.

Since many of us have developed abstract thinking as adults and enjoy the multiple meanings of literature, we sometimes have difficulty accepting that there are men and women worldwide who not only continue to perceive God as a concrete thing and believe in concrete interpretations of scriptures, but also insist that others accept these beliefs. In their dreams of theocratic states, they are adamant that laws should be made according to their concrete interpretations of scriptures. It is amusing that many such people pray to that concrete God as though He, She or It were waiting on the other end of the 1-800 crisis line to change the laws of nature according to the wishes of the caller.

I am intrigued when I hear a heated, angry, even bitter debate between a believer and a non-believer, a religious person and an atheist, when a believer tries to prove and a non-believer tries to disprove a concrete God, both of them failing to realize that they are using concrete thinking for a metaphor. Such discussions usually involve more than an image of God— they usually involve concepts like that of Adam and Eve, or Heaven and Hell. A concrete thinker has a hard time accepting that in Middle Eastern mythology Adam and Eve's story was symbolic of every man and woman on earth, and that Heaven and Hell are states of mind, not places.

I am amused how people who, at one stage of life, believed in the tooth fairy and Santa Claus stopped believing in them as concrete realities by age fifteen but continue to believe in a personal God at the age of fifty. I am also fascinated by adults who have developed metaphorical thinking about God but regress to concrete thinking when they become old and feel vulnerable, or experience an emotional crisis. I think that like individuals, families and communities can also regress, becoming overly religious as they return to concrete thinking about God; they may revert to praying for miracles if they go through a social, economic or political crisis such as a war or famine, or experience a natural disaster like a flood or earthquake. Erica Jong once observed, "There are no atheists on turbulent airplanes." In crises and tragedies such people pray to the same personal and concrete God who they believe sent them that natural disaster. Some even believe that the natural disaster was caused by their sins and that they must repent so that their angry God will become forgiving and merciful.

I am quite aware that while there are non-believers who grow doubtful when experiencing a physical or emotional crisis, there are others who feel so strong in their faith in themselves that they remain committed atheists and humanists even when they are penalized and persecuted.

I think that when humanity reaches the stage of mental growth and cultural evolution when most people can understand scriptures as folklore and not as divine revelations, can view them as mythology rather than stories, and can differentiate facts from fiction, there might be more wisdom and peace and fewer conflicts and holy wars in this world.

22.   SEVEN CAUSES OF HUMAN SUFFERING

In the twenty-first century, humanity is at a crossroads. We have reached a stage of adolescence in our growth as a species. Since the discovery of the atomic bomb, human beings are, for the first time in history, able to commit collective suicide. I hope that rather than following the path of self-destruction, human beings choose to progress to the next stage of evolution and learn to live in peace and harmony with themselves and others. Human beings need to realize that we are intimately connected with each other and to have any collective future we need to work together to decrease our sufferings.

When I review the contemporary dynamics of social, economic and political factors, I can easily recognize the following seven main causes of human suffering.

1. ISSUE OF CLASS

Many of us have grown up in communities where there has been a wide gulf between the rich and the poor. When we talk about upper, middle and lower classes, we acknowledge the gap that exists between the *haves* and the *have-nots*. It is a sad reality that 20% of the world's people own 80% of the resources while the other 80% struggle to exist on the remaining 20%. The differences between developed and developing countries are incredible--the minority enjoys all the luxuries while the majority struggles for food and shelter and cannot afford to educate their children or buy medicine.

The time has come for the *haves* and the *have-nots* at a local, national and international level to realize that we are collectively responsible for the health and well being of all humans and we must adopt a lifestyle where millions of children all over the world will not die of malnutrition, starvation and treatable illnesses. Only with such a realization is there hope that developing countries will be encouraged to be economically and politically self-sufficient and independent. Even in the developed world, on one hand there are countries like Canada whose social support system provides free education and health care to all citizens, while in neighbouring America millions of people have no health insurance and cannot afford medical expenses.

2. ISSUE OF RACE

Alongside class differences, in some communities there exist inequalities between different ethnic groups. One example is South Africa where, for generations, Whites enjoyed far more rights and privileges than Browns and Blacks. The White minority ruled the Black majority. In India there has been a caste system for centuries. Even among Muslims, Syeds were more esteemed than other groups as they were considered to be the descendants of Mohammad. These distinctions focus more on racial and family background than on the character of the person. Such attitudes have led to appalling social injustice. In America, Martin Luther King, Jr. worked hard to change discriminatory laws so that Blacks could be treated equally to Whites.

3. ISSUE OF GENDER

In the past, there existed in some parts of the world matriarchal societies where women were well respected. The expressions *mother tongue* and *motherland* remind us of those times. But in recent centuries human beings have been living in patriarchal societies and women have been considered second-class citizens, deprived of many rights and privileges. The feminist and women's liberation movements have made great strides over the decades but the attitudes of men are so deep-rooted that it might take a few more generations for many men to accept women as equals and to respect them. It is also interesting to note that alongside cultural traditions, there exist religious groups that deny women equal rights. In many religions there can be no women prophets and women cannot lead religious gatherings.

4. ISSUE OF RELIGION

While some people use their religion to become better human beings and serve their communities, there are also those who use it to judge others. They display a punitive attitude and seek to persecute those whom they consider sinners. It is sad to see how many religious groups have split into sects and have declared holy wars on others. Whether they be Shiites fighting with Sunnis in Iraq or Catholics fighting with Protestants in Ireland or Muslims fighting with Jews in Israel, there is a religious motivation in these political wars. It is difficult for many people to rise above their religious and cultural conditioning and embrace people from other faiths and sects as their brothers and sisters, or to respect atheists and humanists, whom they see as sinners who will burn in hell. Equally troubling are theocratic states where leaders use the force of national law to persecute people from minority sects. I think the time has come for all such governments to separate church and state/mosque and state and create secular societies where there is not only freedom *of* religion but also freedom *from* religion.

5. ISSUE OF SEXUAL ORIENTATION

Whenever there is an open and honest debate about the rights of gays and lesbians a number of biases and prejudices surface. In some communities homosexuality is considered immoral, in others—unnatural, in still others—illegal. For centuries, gay men and lesbian women have suffered because of the homophobic attitudes of their communities. It is only recently that some countries are recognizing their right to get married and celebrate their love publicly.

6. ISSUE OF PHYSICAL AND MENTAL DISABILITIES

It is not uncommon to see people with physical and mental disabilities treated poorly by others. As a psychiatrist I am quite aware of the stigma of mental illness. Many face negativity from their families and prejudice in their workplace. The creation of special parking places for people with disabilities in parking areas across Canada is a welcome development. There is also a growing awareness that people with emotional problems and mental illnesses need to be treated compassionately rather than punitively.

7. ISSUE OF NATIONALISM

It is amazing to observe how people develop a strong identity based on the country where they were born. Their feelings of patriotism not only make them love their own country but at times inspire them to declare war on countries they consider their enemies, and if religion is closely linked with patriotism then the war becomes a holy war. Some call it a *jihad* while others call it a *crusade*. It is sad to see how millions of people blindly follow their leaders into a cycle of violence that can continue for generations and which is hard to break.

CONCLUDING REMARKS

When we review all seven causes of human suffering we become aware that some factors affect more human beings than others. For example class issues can affect 80% of the world population, gender issues 50% and sexual orientation issues 10%. Some suffer more than others because they are affected by more than one factor. For example a black working class lesbian woman might struggle on four fronts and suffer multiple disadvantages with overlapping impacts.

A review of Human rights organizations worldwide shows that some committed people focus on the human rights of only one group and overlook others. It is a sad reality that many human beings have been suffering for centuries but now, with the advancement of knowledge in science, medicine, psychology and economics, and the development of a humanistic attitude in many parts of the world, we can solve most human problems. However, this requires people who are committed to their cause and ideals.

The time has come for all individuals, local groups and international organizations who believe in democracy, social justice and peace to rise above their ideological and political differences and work together to serve their communities and create a better future for all of us. Humanity is at a crossroads. Rather than committing collective suicide and perishing as a species I hope we enter the next stage of human evolution and create a secular, humanistic and peaceful world.

23. SEVEN REASONS TO KILL

*Man is the only species that is a mass murderer, the
only misfit in his own society. Why should this be so?*
N. Tribergen.

When angry human beings act violently and aggressively, other caring and compassionate human beings sometimes tell them they are acting like animals. Given the level of violence in the contemporary world, I would not be surprised to hear of some kind animals saying to other cruel animals that they were acting like humans. Eric Fromm in his famous book, *The Anatomy of Human Destructiveness* shares his insight that animals express *benign* violence—they kill only in self-defence or when they are hungry. Even a lion is peaceful when he is not hungry and does not feel threatened. On the other hand, humans are worse than animals as they exhibit *malignant* violence—they add a series of meanings to their violence. They justify their violent crimes and rationalize their aggressive acts. Such justifications are also presented by social groups, political institutions and religious organizations. In communities, cultures and countries where capital punishment is allowed, when one human kills another human, the entire society commits the same crime by killing the killer. "Do human beings individually or collectively have the right to kill other human beings?" is a vital question for the evolution of humanity. Such killings are usually justified by the age old saying, "an eye for an eye". Over the centuries many wise men and women have observed that if we act on this belief, within a short time half the village will be blind.

When we study the history of humanity, we realize the intensity and severity of human violence and aggression has increased over the centuries. In the twentieth century alone, millions of humans have killed others in pre-meditated murder. This includes the use of nuclear weapons. If we review human murders we can classify them into the following seven groups based on emotional, social, religious, economic or political motivation.

1.   PERSONAL REVENGE
There are people in every community who have difficulty controlling their anger. If someone hurts them, rather than

forgiving or reporting the matter to the authorities, they take the law into their own hands. As a psychotherapist I am fascinated by the number of murders that happen within families; people kill those they had loved at one time. Their sense of betrayal transforms their love into hate, and lovers become enemies. Spouses who once vowed eternal love can kill each other because of jealousy. It is sad to see domestic and family violence killing so many people every year, especially children and women.

2.   SERIAL KILLERS

While some kill people they know intimately, there are others who kill strangers. We call them serial killers and mass murderers. I interviewed Javed Iqbal Mughal who had confessed to killing one hundred children in Pakistan. Reviewing the research on serial killers, I was shocked to discover that the United States had the highest number of serial killings in the world. These serial killers, who were usually physically, emotionally and sexually abused as children, became vengeful against a particular group, be they blacks or women, gays or Hispanics, whom they kill indiscriminately until they are caught by police. Many such serial killers have psychopathic and sociopathic personalities.

3.   SOCIAL VIOLENCE OF GANGS

As more and more people move from villages to cities and adopt an urban lifestyle, they face the pains of migration, social alienation and unemployment. Some of them become involved in violent gangs and engage in selling drugs to make quick money. Unfortunately, once they enter the drug and gang culture it is difficult for them to leave. It is fascinating how these gangs provide a sense of identity and belonging to young men and women who feel lost, confused and isolated in big cities. When there are violent confrontations between gangs, we see many murders. In some cases even the local police become involved in these violent crimes.

4.   MENTAL ILLNESS

While the majority of murders are committed by psychopaths who do not suffer from mental illness, some are committed by people suffering from schizophrenia, manic depressive illness and paranoid psychosis. When these emotionally disturbed people feel threatened and attacked, they may think they need to kill before they are killed. Such people, rather than going to prison, are sent to hospitals for psychiatric treatment.

5. POLITICAL / NATIONAL VIOLENCE

As the concept of nationalism became popular in the West, states created national armies. Over the centuries, soldiers in the uniform of one country killed only the soldiers of the enemy army. With the rise of guerrilla warfare, both sides participate in the slaughter of innocent men, women and children. Some call it using human shields while others call it collateral damage. Innocent citizens are killed with no twinge of conscience on either side.

Human beings can be executed by their own governments, under capital punishment laws ordered by the courts. These are murders committed by legalized state violence.

6. VIOLENCE OF RELIGIOUS FUNDAMENTALISTS

Over the centuries, believers have killed each other in the name of God. In the last few decades there have been a large number of killings between Sunnis and Shiites, Catholics and Protestants, Hindus and Muslims, and Muslims and Jews in different parts of the world. Ironically, these violent murders are committed in the name of a merciful God. Some are done to create theocratic states. Many such murders are ordered by religious leaders who have charismatic and cultish personalities.

7. INTERNATIONAL VIOLENCE

In the recent past, Western governments have sent their armies to other countries for the purpose of invading sovereign states in order to topple their governments; they have killed innocent civilians and rationalized their murder in the name of democracy, human rights and freedom. These are economic wars, aimed at establishing the aggressor's military presence all over the world, selling weapons and ensuring access to the conquered countries' resources.

CONCLUDING COMMENTS

It is sad to realize that violent consciousness is on the rise and that the borders between just and unjust wars have blurred. Even in the twenty-first century we have not risen above a tribal mentality. I am afraid that if we do not develop peace consciousness and do not feel compassion for all of humanity, we might commit collective suicide and may not evolve to the next stage of human evolution.

It is ironic that, in the contemporary world, leaders of religious, spiritual and secular traditions claim their ideologies and philosophies promote peace while their followers continue to kill each other. Whether they are followers of Christianity or Islam, Judaism or Hinduism, Communism or Capitalism, they kill innocent human beings and justify their murders through religion and ideology.

I think the time has come for all of us to learn to communicate better and find ways to resolve our personal, social, religious and political conflicts peacefully and respectfully, and accept that killing one human is like killing all of humanity.

24.   FROM TRIBALISM TO HUMANISM

In the distant past, human beings lived a primitive lifestyle. Dwelling in caves and jungles, they hunted to survive. Because of limited resources, they were vulnerable to malnutrition and starvation or to sudden death from natural disasters or attacks by wild animals. For their survival and growth, they lived in small tribes whose members protected each other. While the men hunted with their arrows and spears, the women looked after the children and animals. Such a lifestyle created an *us and them* tribal mentality. Each tribe saw other tribes as potential enemies who would attack them and steal their women, children and animals. To protect their limited resources, they were always prepared for tribal wars. Killing members of another tribe could start a tribal war that continued for generations, in which innocent men, women and children were killed for revenge. Sometimes the goal was not only to kill but to humiliate. Rather than dispatching their enemies quickly, they would torture them so that they died a painful and humiliating death.

In the last few thousand years human beings have made progress in many aspects of life but in some areas their thinking and attitudes remain primitive. In the twenty-first century, human beings may live in skyscrapers in huge cities, travel in cars, trains and planes, and communicate around the planet by telephone and internet as members of a worldwide global village. But many have neither evolved in their minds nor grown in their personalities. They still have a tribal mentality—all that has changed is the definition of the tribe and the nature of tribal war.

To understand the dynamics of modern tribal war we need to understand the psychology of the tribal mental set. How does such a war start and how is the cycle of violence initiated and maintained?

Analysis of such wars shows they can be started by a person, a group, an organization or an institution. The details differ but there are some common characteristics in such people, organizations and institutions.

The person who starts the modern tribal war

...feels threatened, insecure or vulnerable, or identifies with a bereaved party

...emotionally identifies with a tribe, a herd, a group

...gets into an *us and them* mental set and perceives the *other* as an enemy

...attacks the enemy to take revenge or prevent future attacks

If the opponent has a similar tribal mental set, the tribal war and the cycle of violence may continue for days, weeks, months, years, decades, generations, even centuries.

A cycle of violence and tribal war can take place between two ordinary people and their families, or two heads of state, or two leaders of organizations or institutions who perceive each other as enemies or potential enemies.

Such an *us and them* division can be triggered on the basis of:

Religion...Jews, Muslims, Christians, Hindus

Sects...Shiites and Sunnis in Muslims, Catholics and Protestants in Christians.

Race...Blacks and Whites

Gender...Men and Women

Language...French and English, Urdu and Bengali

Sexual Orientation...Homosexuals and heterosexuals

Nationality...Indians and Pakistanis, Americans and Iraqis

As the war continues, both enemies pass on their tribal mental set to the next generation who, once brainwashed, join the tribal war started by their elders and previous generations. It is tragic to see that when the cycle of violence continues and tribal war is maintained, people on both sides start identifying with the opponent to acquire the psychological profile of the enemy. They begin to mirror each other's personality and political strategy in order to fight fire with fire. Compared to those with a tribal mental set, people who are emotionally, socially and culturally evolved have acquired a Humanistic mental set and developed a Humanistic Personality. For such people, their primary identity is that of *human being*. They might have other identities based on religion, race, language, gender, sexual orientation or nationality, but those identities remain secondary, and whenever there is a conflict between primary and secondary identities, they think, feel and act according to the primary identity. This Humanistic philosophy and personality helps them maintain a rational and cooperative attitude rather than irrational and confrontational one. It enables them to transcend the *us and them* mentality and encourages them to resolve conflicts with people from other social and cultural backgrounds. They focus more on similarities than differences. Their philosophy creates a peaceful lifestyle at a personal and social level rather than involvement in war at a political level.

It is unfortunate that even in the twenty-first century, many of us still have a primitive tribal person sleeping in our unconscious mind and when we feel threatened and vulnerable the sleeping tribal person wakes up and joins the tribe emotionally, socially and politically to fight a tribal war.

On the evening news we see multiple examples of tribal wars fought on religious grounds, such as the conflict between Christians and Muslims when Pope Benedict criticized Muslims, and on political and economic grounds between Americans and Iraqis because of the holy oil. Be they American soldiers or Iraqi guerrilla warriors, they rationalize killing thousands of innocent men, women and children on the basis of tribe against tribe. On an international level, economic wars are waged as colonial powers loot the resources of poor and vulnerable countries. Some of the latter, although weak and starving, are trying to create nuclear weapons to protect themselves against contemporary pre-emptive tribal wars.

As we become more aware of our unconscious tribal mentality and consciously adopt a humanistic philosophy, we will be able to rise above our differences, resolve our conflicts at a personal, social and political level, and learn to live with each other harmoniously and peacefully. Loving one's neighbour has been a part of folk wisdom for centuries—we just need to broaden the definition of neighbour to include all races and all tribes, as we are now, more than ever, living in a global village. We need to help our children to develop the primary identity of human beings and rise above the tribal mentality based on race, colour, language, gender, nationalism and religion. Those identities, which unite their members at a small, self-protective sub-group level, divide us as members of the global human family.

Given the arsenal of nuclear weapons in the world, we are quite capable of committing collective suicide if we do not accept the philosophy of humanism. Such a philosophy will help us become fully human, individually and collectively. Every human being has to do some introspection and rise above the tribal mentality to embrace all of humanity.

A few years ago I wrote a poem reflecting my humanistic philosophy:

WE ARE ALL CHILDREN OF MOTHER EARTH

When will we realize?
We share the same ancestors
Our enemies are our distant cousins
Alienated by ethnic and religious walls
Separated by linguistic and national borders
Divided by the history of Holy Wars
When will we become aware?
We all belong to the same race
  The same tribe
    The same family
      The Human family

We all share
  The same moon
    The same sun
      The same mountains
        The same valleys
          The same deserts
            The same jungles
              The same winds
                The same oceans

When will we recognize?
We are all children of Mother Earth

Dr. K Sohail

25. THE ROLE OF MYSTICS, ARTISTS AND SCIENTISTS IN HUMAN EVOLUTION

When we study human history, we realize that human beings have been evolving over centuries. In every generation there was a majority that blindly followed traditional beliefs and practices. Such traditions gave birth to religions whose leaders gained power in their communities, ruling the masses by directing their personal and social lives. Some of those leaders became intoxicated with power and began misguiding their communities socially, economically and politically. As those religions and traditions became more institutionalized, the abuse of power increased. But in every generation there was also a minority of creative personalities, whether mystics, artists or scientists, who questioned those traditions and challenged those religious leaders.

Through the centuries, there have been many mystics from different cultural traditions, be they sufis or sadhus, sants or saints, who followed their own hearts rather than the highway of tradition. Perceived as threats to religious and political establishments, these mystics were labelled heretics and were penalized, persecuted, even executed, because they were sympathetic to common people. Kabir Das, Bullay Shah, Sheikh Saadi, Maulana Rumi, William Blake, and Walt Whitman all challenged the religious and social traditions of their time and paid a heavy price. Mansoor Hallaj, the famous mystic, was crucified for saying *analhaq [I am truth]*. Many priests, rabbis, maulanas and pundits,the privileged religious elites of their communities, feel threatened by these mystics who accept rather than judge people. Common people always loved, respected and cherished the mystics of their communities who were not concerned with the concepts of sin and guilt and burning in hell but instead, led simple lives and served their communities. Mystics established the value of human experience and personal truth over traditional beliefs and scriptures. Their philosophy can be summarized by the sayings of two mystics. Buddha, the ancient mystic said,
" Believe nothing just because a so-called wise person said it
Believe nothing just because a belief is generally held
Believe nothing just because it is said in ancient books
Believe nothing just because it is said to be of divine origin

Believe nothing just because someone else believes it
Believe only what you yourself test and judge to be true."

The modern mystic of twentieth century, J Krishnamurti stated, "Truth is a pathless land"

As humanity evolved, many creative personalities who challenged traditional beliefs became artists. They developed different forms of expression, creating poems, plays and paintings to challenge traditional morality. Endowed with rich imaginations and non-traditional ways of seeing the world they suggested that scriptures were part of folklore and wisdom literature, and that we need metaphorical rather than literal interpretations of holy books. Artists connected with the masses at an emotional level and inspired them to challenge traditional morality based on scriptures. Traditional religious leaders and institutions challenged by mystics felt threatened by artists whom they penalized and persecuted.

Artists redefine our concept of good based on aesthetic rather than moral values. Artists help us to appreciate the beauty of nature and humanity and to get in touch with our inner beauty. They help us develop our Right Brains in order to appreciate words, colours and sounds and, in doing so, touch the artist inside all of us. They keep alive our inner child who loves to play and enjoy life. In our stressful lives full of family, work and social responsibilities, artists help us enter an imaginary world where we enjoy their creative products. Whether they are the plays of Shakespeare and Ibsen, the paintings of Picasso and Van Gogh, the novels of Virginia Woolf and Franz Kafka or the poems of Mirza Ghalib and Pablo Neruda, they inspire us and we find them entertaining as well as enlightening. The creation of art and literature has been a major step in human evolution.

In the last few centuries, human beings have crossed another milestone in evolution through the disciplines of Science and Philosophy. Scientists question not only religious leaders, but also mystics and artists. Scientists insist on logical and rational proof before they accept anything. Scientists believe that there are two kinds of truth, subjective truth and objective truth. For any truth to be accepted universally it has to be proved to others. In the last couple of centuries, scientists and philosophers have explored different aspects of life—biology, psychology, economics, sociology— and the discoveries of Charles Darwin, Karl Marx and Albert Einstein have changed how we see ourselves, other human beings and the universe around us.

It appears as though mystics and artists challenged religious traditions from the inside while philosophers and scientists attacked them from outside. While mystics and artists helped human beings to develop their Right Brains, scientists and philosophers stimulated the growth and evolution of the Left Brain. In the twentieth century, writings of scientists and philosophers like Bertrand Russell, Jean Paul Sartre, Sigmund Freud and Stephen Hawking took the rational understanding of human life and the universe to new heights and depths and emphasized that human beings can solve their personal and social problems without the need for God, religion, scriptures and divine revelations.

As the disciplines of science and philosophy have grown, not only have human minds developed but also human communities. In schools, colleges and universities education is based on scientific values, while at the state level, laws have been made on secular and humanistic principles.

Scientists and philosophers remain mentally prepared to follow the tradition of Socrates, who was condemned to drink poison for inspiring young people to question their religious and cultural traditions.

In the twentieth century, many humanistic psychologists studied creative and mystic encounters from a secular and scientific point of view. People like William James and Julian Jaynes broadened the horizons of human psychology, attempting to prove that our spirituality is part of our humanity rather than part of divinity. Abraham Maslow proved that to have peak experiences (creative and mystic experiences) human beings need not believe in any God or organized religion. Such experiences are more related to the stimulation of the Right Temporal Lobes; they are products of the human unconscious mind rather than of gods and angels. These psychologists developed a secular discipline of human psychology, following a humanistic tradition in which our understanding of the human mind and personality is based on our scientific and secular principles rather than holy scriptures.

As we review communities around the world in the twenty-first century we become aware that many are still guided by religious traditions where religious leaders have wide-ranging social, economic and political powers. These leaders still demand the practice of their brand of holy scriptures in everyone's personal and political lives, and insist on theocratic states deriving laws from holy scriptures on which no two sects agree. On the other hand, there are communities where religion has become a private concern, and social and legal matters are guided by secular, scientific and humanistic values.

I am of the opinion that blind faith and religion were our past and science, psychology and philosophy are our future as human beings. On the journey of human evolution we are gradually evolving from religious communities and theocratic states to secular communities and humanistic states where all citizens will enjoy equal rights and privileges. On this journey mystics, artists, scientists and philosophers, with their personal, creative and rational truths have been paving the way for social change over the centuries and paying a heavy price for challenging age-old traditions. In spite of their differences, they worked towards human liberation, focusing on personal truth, creative imagination and rational thinking. All these groups have reformed their communities, enacting social change by challenging blind faith and inspiring people to achieve social consciousness and enlightenment. Mystics, artists, philosophers and scientists, they all suffered, but their sufferings paved a way for future growth. They blazed their own trails and these trails have become highways for future generations.

Creative people have always been a minority but that minority has been leading the majority on the journey to human evolution. Arnold Toynbee, a famous historian, once wrote,

"To give a fair chance to potential creativity is a matter of life and death for any society. This is all-important, because the outstanding creative ability of a fairly small percentage of the population is mankind's ultimate capital asset. (ref p113 "The Nature of Creativity: Contemporary Psychological Perspectives" edited by Robert J. Sternberg, Robert J Phd Sternberg)"

26.　SEVEN HUMANIST PHILOSOPHERS

SECULAR ETHICS

After my lecture at the Humanist Association of Toronto last month, one of the presenters asked me, "If you do not believe in God, prophets, religions, divine revelations, the concept of sin and the Day of Judgment, then as atheists, agnostics, freethinkers and humanists, where do you get your guidance from? What is the source of your morality?" Whenever I am asked that question by believers, whether Muslims, Christians or Jews, I share with them that over the centuries, human beings have reached a stage in their evolution where the human psyche (mind and personality) has developed a personal and social conscience. Such a conscience does not need divine revelations to guide it. I share with them that throughout history, in every community and in every century, there have been philosophers who have sought to articulate humanist philosophy.

In the twenty-first century, human beings have choices. They can follow the religious traditions of Moses, Jesus and Mohammad that gave birth to monotheistic religions in the Middle East, and which provide guidelines for religious morality dictated by divine revelation and holy scripture; or they can follow the secular ethics and humanist philosophy shared by secular psychologists and humanist philosophers. Since the list of those philosophers is very long, in this essay I will focus on the ethical principles presented by only seven humanist philosophers from different areas of the world: China, India, Greece, Europe and North America.

1. CONFUCIUS

A study of modern human history reveals that the first humanist philosopher was Confucius, who lived in China from 551 BC to 479 BC. He was the first to present reciprocity as the fundamental principle of secular philosophy. His principle, known as the Golden Rule or the Silver Rule, states: *don't do to others what you wouldn't want done to you.* Confucius can be called the Father of Humanist Philosophy. He presented the principle that right things should be done for right reasons. He believed that human beings are good by nature and that we need to respect them and help them be virtuous, rather than perceiving them as sinners and evil and controlling their behaviour through fear of punishment. Confucius was so respected by his community that he was asked to become Minister of Justice, through which position he carried out many reforms in China. His advice to the leaders of the state was to rule by example. He expected them to live by the same ethical principles they wanted their subjects to follow.

2. BUDDHA

The second secular philosopher was Buddha who, most historians agree, lived in India from 563 BC to 483 BC. He was known as Siddhartha until he achieved enlightenment and was then revered as Buddha, The Enlightened One. He challenged the prevalent religious superstitions, dogmas, morals and authorities, and taught people to trust their own heart, their own conscience, their own inner wisdom. He said,

Believe nothing just because a so-called wise person said it.
Believe nothing just because a belief is generally held.
Believe nothing just because it is said in ancient books.
Believe nothing just because it is said to be of divine origin.
Believe nothing just because someone else believes it.
Believe only what you yourself test and judge to be true.

Buddha believed that *"one's own experience is the best teacher."* He helped people to live a healthy, happy and peaceful life by following the path designated by their conscience, and by treating others with compassion.

3. HIPPOCRATES

The third humanist philosopher was Hippocrates, known as the Father of Secular Medicine. He was born on the Greek island of Kos in 460 BC and lived for nearly 100 years. He was the first physician to separate medicine from religion and the first to focus on the importance of finding the natural causes of human suffering. Hippocrates observed that when people became physically sick, some believed that they had sinned and that the gods were punishing them. This required sacrifices to please the gods. Others believed that they were possessed by demons. Hippocrates questioned religious beliefs of sin and guilt, and challenged prevalent superstitions. He presented alternate secular theories, and based on his clinical observations and experiences, proved that human ailments were related to faulty diet, lack of exercise, poor sleep and unhealthy lifestyles. He suggested to his patients that, rather than praying and offering sacrifices to the gods, they should try to eat a balanced diet, engage in regular exercise, sleep better and adopt a healthy lifestyle to improve their quality of life.

Hippocrates also suggested an oath for physicians, known as the Hippocratic Oath. He emphasized that if physicians cannot help, at least they need to take care not to hurt their patients. In his own clinical practice Hippocrates was reluctant to use remedies if he was not sure of their effectiveness. Over the centuries, the Hippocratic Oath has remained a guide for all schools and colleges of physicians, regulating the secular ethics of their members and exhorting them to maintain a high standard of medical practice.

4. SOCRATES

The fourth humanist philosopher was Socrates, who lived from 469 BC to 399 BC. One of his many students, Plato, presented the wisdom he learnt from him in his *Socratic Dialogues*. Socrates loved to challenge the traditions of his community and culture and engage with his young followers in passionate dialogues about life. He was criticized, persecuted and finally charged with two crimes: corrupting the minds of the younger generation with his secular philosophy and not believing in the gods of the state. He was found guilty and ordered to drink poison, which he gladly did to uphold his honour and integrity.

Socrates promoted rational, logical and analytical thinking and inspired his students and disciples to challenge religious authority, dogma and superstitions. He believed that the unexamined life was not worth living and that human beings discover truth through dialogue. Socrates believed in living an honest, sincere and ethical life. Even at the time of his death he asked his student not to forget to pay his debt.

Socrates taught a dialectic method of inquiry, now known as the Socratic method, which has become one of the bases of Western philosophy and science. Such a method is used to discover secular values of goodness and justice rather than relying on divine revelations. Socrates helped humans to discover their truth in their personal and social lives and create secular laws to run the state. Rather than accepting the concept of sin, he helped humanity to adopt the concept of just laws.

Socrates has become the Father of Western Secular Philosophy.

5. SIGMUND FREUD

The fifth humanist philosopher was Sigmund Freud, who had a strong interest in human psychology. He lived in Europe from 1856 to 1939. Freud developed the discipline of psychoanalysis and attempted to solve the riddles of the human unconscious mind by analyzing dreams, jokes and other unusual human behaviours. He analyzed how the religious beliefs of childhood can become part of a harsh super-ego and contribute to human suffering. Rather than judging people on religious morals, he encouraged people to understand the dynamics of mental health and illness. He presented a hierarchy of defense and coping mechanisms, showing how healthy people use healthy mechanisms (for example humour and sublimation) to deal with the dilemmas of life, while unhealthy people who suffer from emotional problems and mental illnesses use unhealthy coping mechanisms (for example, denial, acting out and projection). He observed that many neurotic people use the defence mechanism of rationalization, giving rational reasons for their emotionally motivated behaviours. He helped his patients resolve their emotional conflicts and learn healthy coping mechanisms. Freud promoted a secular and scientific attitude rather than a religious and dogmatic outlook. He believed that, as the borders of science expanded, the frontiers of religion would shrink.

6. VICTOR FRANKL

The sixth humanist philosopher was Victor Frankl, a European psychotherapist who lived from 1905 to 1997. His book, Man's Search for Meaning, based on his experiences as a holocaust survivor, has been translated into more than twenty languages. He was a strong promoter of secular ethics. He developed a mode of therapy called logo-therapy, which focuses on how human beings can better deal with their suffering if they discover a meaning in it. Frankl encouraged people to find their own meaning in life and was a source of inspiration for millions.

7. ABRAHAM MASLOW

The seventh humanist philosopher was Abraham

Maslow, an American psychologist who lived from 1908 to 1970. He is well-known for his book *Motivation and Personality*, in which he described a hierarchy of needs. He believed that at the lowest level, people are motivated by the basic human needs of hunger and thirst. People living at a higher lever are motivated by the need for security and self esteem; and people living at the highest level of mental health and maturity are motivated by their self-actualizing needs. He calls the last group *self-actualized people*. Such people get in touch with their creative potential and become poets and philosophers, artists and mystics, reformers and revolutionaries and take their communities to the next stage of human evolution. Maslow also had a keen interest in religious and spiritual experiences. He believed that these were human experiences and that people did not need to believe in any God or religion to have them. He called them *peak experiences.* As a psychologist he offered explanations of such spiritual encounters that are accepted by clergy as well as atheists. He believed that spirituality is part of humanity, rather than divinity.

Over the centuries, secular philosophers and humanist psychologists have been laying the foundations of secular ethics and humanist philosophy. In the twenty-first century, people have a choice: to follow the traditions of monotheistic religions or adopt the secular traditions of modern science and psychology, medicine and philosophy.

In the last couple of centuries the number of people following the secular tradition has been increasing. In 1900 the number of atheists and agnostics, freethinkers and humanists was 1% worldwide. In 2000 the number had increased to 15%. In Canada the number is 19% and in Scandinavian countries, more than 50%

One of the accomplishments of secular humanism is to replace religious laws with secular laws and the concept of sin with that of crime. In secular states, people who commit crimes are not punished by religious laws and sent to hell; rather, they are judged by an impartial judicial system and helped by compassionate psychologists and psychiatrists who create rehabilitation programs for such people. Secular-minded people are creating secular humanist states where all citizens have equal rights and privileges, especially women and minorities. The *International Declaration of Human Rights* by the United

Nations in 1948 has been a major milestone in providing a framework for secular ethics and laws. Many primarily religious countries are gradually transforming themselves into secular humanist states where people are following secular ethics in their personal, social and political lives.

PART FIVE

Reviews

27. GOODBYE ISLAM, HELLO HUMANISM
by Gabrielle Bauer

Dr. Khalid Sohail has traveled through space, time and belief systems to reach the secular spiritualism that now informs his psychiatry practice

When Whitby, Ont., psychiatrist Dr. Khalid Sohail wrote his book *From Islam to Secular Humanism*, he had no idea that the religion of his birth would soon be under global scrutiny. Nor did he realize that his book would surface amid a flurry of media discussions that challenged Islam to defend itself against the charges of extremism and fanaticism.

Dr. Sohail's personal odyssey exemplifies the very opposite of extremism. As outlined in his book, his spiritual evolution has been toward increasingly fluid beliefs and increasing tolerance of all people.

Born in a region of Pakistan that borders Afghanistan, Dr. Sohail describes his family of origin as traditional and devout Muslims. In his early years, he too believed the political and religious tenets he grew up with. "I considered the Hindus to be enemies," he admits. And in his book, he writes that "many times I arose at 3 a.m. in the darkness of early morning . . . to pray to God to convert the entire world to Islam."

But the road less traveled beckoned to Dr. Sohail during his teenage years, when he began to study science. Attracted not only to scientific facts but to the "scientific attitude," which he saw as contradictory to the religious philosophy he had been imbued with from birth, he found himself in a state of mounting inner conflict that reached a climax during his university years. "Eventually, science won out," he says. "I realized there was no turning back to what I had been and believed."

Dr. Sohail's creative juices also began flowing during that time. He wrote numerous poems and short stories, publishing them in university periodicals. "I actually wanted to become a poet," he says with a chuckle. But his mother, like mothers the world over, posed the question: "And how will you live?" She advised medicine, and he acquiesced.

But even when he attended medical school in Pakistan, the poems didn't stop. To the contrary, they became bolder and more controversial. In one of his poems, "The Red Circle," he described the mental turmoil of a pregnant woman who wanted to have an abortion. Another poem he called "Lesbian." "I used the English word because there was no equivalent in my language," he says.

He published several books of poetry and nonfiction, and found a small circle of like-minded spiritual seekers.

Still, Dr. Sohail realized he would always be an outsider in Pakistan or Iran, and that his future lay elsewhere. Deciding on psychiatry as a specialty because "it combines art and science," he applied to residency programs all over the world. He was accepted at a Newfoundland Memorial Universtiy, which is how he ended up in Canada.

When he first settled in his adopted country, Dr. Sohail recalls being confused by the concept of given and family names. "Where I grew up, we don't have first and last names— we just keep adding names on to people," he says. On one occasion, a hospital administrator asked him for his Christian name. Thoroughly mystified, Dr. Sohail ran through his various names in his mind, then answered, "Mohammed."

From Newfoundland, Dr. Sohail moved to a Whitby psychiatric hospital, where he concluded that the currently fashionable neurobiological approach to psychiatry was too concrete for his tastes. He moved on to psychotherapy, attracted by the "humanistic and spiritual element" of the discipline. " 'Psyche' means 'soul,' after all," he says.

Five years ago, Dr. Sohail joined the Creative Psychotherapy practice in Whitby, where he has been practising ever since. Although he treats numerous individual patients, his main focus is on marital therapy. "I'm interested more in the dynamics between people than in people as separate entities," he explains. "Perhaps it's the influence of my Eastern background."

As for his own marital status, it's resolutely single. "I think very few people can combine a creative life with a family life," he says. "At some point I decided to devote myself fully to the creative life." When not treating patients, he spends his time lecturing, writing and making documentaries under the umbrella of his film-production company, Darvesh Films Canada. He also enjoys the company of a wide circle of friends, which he calls his "family of the heart."

Since the publication of his book, Dr. Sohail says about 50 Muslims have contacted him to say they agree with his secular views. "But not in public," he says. Although he downplays the courage it took to go public about his own beliefs, he admits he doesn't know anyone else who has done the same. "People are scared they'll be perceived as traitors and shunned from their community, that they won't be able to marry off their daughters."

While Dr. Sohail himself has no daughters to marry off, he still has numerous relatives in Pakistan. He says they give him and his writings mixed reviews. "The younger generation— my nieces and nephews—is somewhat more open to what I have to say," he says. As for his generational peers, Dr. Sohail says "they're a little embarrassed. They don't quite know what to make of me."

Vocal not only on the subject of his religious non-beliefs, Dr. Sohail has plenty to say about the military activity following the Sept. 11 attacks. What strikes him is how both the U.S. and the Taliban used the same language to describe their enemies. "It's tribal thinking on both sides," he says. "It's just more of the us-and-them mentality, which has never got us anywhere."

As a humanist, Dr. Sohail believes in ferreting out similarities, rather than differences, between people. It's an attitude he brings to his practice, where he tries to help couples bridge their surface differences. "If we all realized we were part of the same human family," he says, "neither couples nor countries would be putting so much energy into fighting with each other."

Gabrielle Bauer is a Toronto writer.

28. *VERUM, IPSUM, FACTUM*
by Munir Saami

May 22, 2010
Review of Dr. Khalid Sohail's book The Next Stage of Human Evolution

For many years, Sohail has focused on learning, understanding, discovering, and contemplation of the human mind, freedoms, liberation, and the never-ending quest for truth behind the complex and ever evolving universe.

Reading the various essays collected in this latest volume, we find a central archetype, a recurring principle that Sohail's writings and creation revolve around in a centripetal and logo centric manner. By logo centric I mean a "foundational presence of Logos or "reason" obtained from an origin of all knowledge (e.g., God or the universe)".

The centre of Sohail's thought has always been the discovery of the "Truth" behind the evolution of the universe and human mind. His thoughts and creation have always spiralled around this centre in various changing orbits, and are never centrifugal; meaning that he never allows his work to flee away from the centre that is the quest for truth.

The success of any writer of fictional or non-fictional narratives is that these narratives should provoke the 'enlightened' reader to pursue further understanding of the themes and principles the writer has presented.

The quest for understanding truth is eternal and as Sohail has suggested; "Highly evolved human beings with creative personalities, whether scientists or artists, poets or philosophers, reformers or revolutionaries, have been trying guide other human beings to the next stage of human evolution by helping them to think critically and logically, imagine creatively, and interact compassionately".

In the above quoted paragraph he, either consciously or by Freudian slip, leaves out the mystics and prophets as those who are also eternally engaged in the search and presentation of truth as per their own understanding or as a divine message that may carry a 'Great Code' or 'Words with Power'. When we undertake the journey towards the principles of humanism, we cannot bypass the Christian humanism of Erasmus, or contemporary religious humanism that many Unitarian-Universalist congregations profess.

Sohail's fundamental search for truth led me to the great 17th century Italian philosopher Giambattista Vico, who presented the principles of *verum esse ipsum factum*, or simply *Verum Factum*, meaning that "truth itself is constructed", and *verum et factum convertuntur*, (the true and the made are convertible).

Vico's works in general, and his principle of *Verum Ipsum Factum,* have influenced writers and philosophers over centuries, including Goethe, Marx, Hegel, James Joyce, William Yeats, Samuel Beckett, Bertrand Russell, Edward Said, Marshal McLuhan, and others. "Hegel and Marx were among the early proponents of the premise that truth is, or can be, socially constructed. Marx, like many critical theorists who followed, did not reject the existence of objective truth but rather distinguished between true knowledge and knowledge that has been distorted through power or ideology."

Vico emphasizes that science should be conceived as the "genus or mode by which a thing is made" so that human science in general is a matter of dissecting the "anatomy of nature's works" albeit through the "vice" of human beings that they are limited to "abstraction" as opposed to the power of "construction" which is found in God alone.

Given that "the norm of the truth is to have made it", Vico reasons, Descartes' famous first principle that clear and distinct ideas are the source of truth must be rejected: "For the mind does not make itself as it gets to know itself," Vico observes, "and since it does not make itself, it does not know the genus or mode by which it makes itself". Thus the truths of morality, natural science, and mathematics do not require "metaphysical justification" as the Cartesians held, but demand an analysis of the causes—the "activity" through which things are made."

Understanding Vico's ideas helps us understand Sohail's discussion on the next stage of human evolution. Nella Cotruppi in her essay, Vico and the Making of Truth, discusses the nature/culture dichotomy, "namely, how are we to understand the transition of humanity from a state of nature to a state of culture or civilization?" She leads us to what Northrop Frye has termed "creative alienation".

In, "Creation and Recreation" Frye suggests, "One can see the importance, for poets and others, of the remoteness and otherness of nature: the feeling that the eighteenth century expressed in the word 'sublime' conveys to us that there is such a thing as creative alienation. The principle laid down by the Italian philosopher Vico of *verum factum*, that we understand only what we have made ourselves, needs to be refreshed sometimes by the contemplation of something we did not make and do not understand."

Contemplation of something we did not make and do not understand leads us to God who for many, on the path of knowledge, is the creator, and who for many is also the custodian and possessor of all that is Truth. In order to understand this creator and holder of the Great Code and the Words with Power, we need to understand ourselves.

This was clearly suggested by the prophet of Islam, whom many hundred years ago, before Vico, Frye, and Sohail said, *"man 'arafa nafsahu faqad 'arafa Rabbahu"*, only he who understands himself, can understand his lord or God.

I am certain that in our discovery of self, we can apply the three C's that Sohail has proposed: Critical Thinking, Creative Imagination, and Compassionate Heart.

To understand the next stage of human evolution we may look into the summation of Vichian ideas, "that man evolves, and not just biologically but in terms of language, custom, social organization, law, and literature. And under all of that lay a bigger time-bomb: that religion itself evolves. Thus

Dr. K Sohail

Vico helped also the advent of doubt", that provokes all inquiry.

Towards the end of his book Sohail expresses the desire of "Creating a Peaceful World Together". This desire resonates with what Vico wrote in his New Science: "There must, in the nature of human institutions, be a mental language common to all nations, which uniformly grasps the substance of things feasible in human social life and expresses it with as many diverse modifications as these same things may have diverse aspects."

References

• Giambattista Vico; New Science (Penguin Classics), 2000
• Caterina Nella Cotrupi; Northrop Frye and the Poetics of Process; University of Toronto Press, Toronto,2000
• Northrop Frye: Creation and Recreation; University of Toronto Press, Toronto, 1980
• Peter Watson: Ideas – A History from Fire to Freud; Phoenix, London, 2005
• May, Todd, 1993, Between Genealogy and Epistemology: Psychology, politics in the thought of Michel Foucault' with reference to Althusser and Balibar, 1970
• http://en.wikipedia.org/wiki/Truth

29. THE NEXT STAGE OF HUMAN EVOLUTION
by Farzana Hasan

I'd like to begin by talking a bit about my first meeting with Dr. Sohail, and how our discussions about religion, philosophy, sociology, and humanism, led me to the surprising realization that despite our being on opposite sides of the religious divide, there existed a significant commonality of thought between us. My views have, to borrow his use of the term, evolved since that time. When I first met him, I informed him that I had rejected traditional understandings of Islam and had developed my own "homegrown" understanding of my faith. Quickly, he asked me what I meant by "homegrown" even though all along, he knew the answer. It is found in his own book, which eloquently describes a religious outlook that falls somewhat in between religious dogmatism and atheism. The first is associated with organized religion. The second represents a clean break from religion. Dr. Sohail had gone through this stage of spiritual evolution himself, as described in the chapter of his book entitled From Fundamentalism to Humanism.

As I read along, I could not help but conclude that he exhibits a keen understanding of comparative religions and successfully relates his findings to his own conclusions. The book is very readable. The author discusses novel ideas like "self transcendence "with depth and clarity in layman's terminology. In fact, the book introduces quite a number of new and interesting ideas. For example, it elaborates on the idea of human spirituality. Traditionally, we have viewed the notion of spirituality as being associated with the "supernatural" or metaphysical, but the author tells us that this need not be the case. Human or earthly spirituality he says, can be understood as a human experience that lifts human beings out of their mundane existence to higher levels of consciousness and self-awareness. Some intense and powerful emotions, like love, can take human beings to newer heights of ecstasy. In thus discussing human spirituality, Dr Sohail elucidates the philosophy of the mystic/psychotherapist Victor Frankl.

When I look at my own philosophical evolution, and that

of Dr Sohail's as described in his own book, I see many parallels. The book in fact describes how collective evolution toward a humanistic identity can take place one individual at a time. This is possible whether one is a religious humanist or a secular humanist. This "next stage of human evolution" will result in societies that are more humane, more egalitarian and more tolerant. The practical steps to achieve this noble goal will require an acknowledgement of the primacy of our common humanity, as opposed to the ascendancy of superficial differences based on culture, ethnicity or religion. Although the book is a collection of essays written at different times for different occasions, the theme that human beings must evolve to achieve a better, more harmonious world is apparent to the reader.

Borrowing the word evolution from the person who used it most efficiently, Dr Sohail begins the book by discussing Charles Darwin's role in shaping a new way of thinking. Indeed, Darwin is credited with turning the world from a theistic to a more humanistic world, by formulating a theory of man's origin rooted in the natural rather than the spiritual realm. Darwin as presented by Dr. Sohail favours critical thought as opposed to blind faith.

He writes: Darwin's theory of evolution has forced millions of people over the world to review their beliefs about god, scriptures, creation and the special position of man in the universe. Those who welcome scientific research have changed their positions. Over the decades the numbers of scientists, biologists, intellectuals, and lay people who believe in the theory of evolution is increasing."

When I read this, I thought about how this was linked to the idea of the next stage of human evolution described by the author as humanism. The connection is quite straightforward. We are all forced to recognize our humble origins, rather than blindly accept fanciful ideas of having descended from gods, or of being the chosen of God.

Within this context, I noticed Dr Sohail urging humanity to set some goals for itself. The goal is peace, harmony and cooperation among all human beings—one that has until now, remained elusive. Toward achieving this goal, the author discusses Joseph Campbell and uses a very interesting analogy to describe his philosophical style. I can detect the poet Sohail in these lines. On page 40 he says: "Campbell was like a mythological old man, sitting on the top of a mountain watching the caravans of humanity."

He points out that Campbell exemplified a humanistic personality, as he was a kind man who accepted rather than judged humanity. He further states that Campbell was a gentle and compassionate man—a quality, if instilled in human beings universally, would eventually lead to better, more humane communities. Dr Sohail also notes that Campbell is a unifier between eastern and western thought, and alludes to the possibility of reconciling the two traditions. He also envisions the possibility of the Eastern and Western traditions enriching each other. I must say here that the author's commentary on various philosophers is a faithful and insightful depiction of their philosophical thought—a quality that can be seen throughout the book.

In the chapter entitled "The Psychology of spiritual Encounters" Dr. Sohail chronicles his own spiritual transformation. It was in this chapter that I encountered some of the most lucid expositions of the philosophies of spiritual figures like Krishanmurti, the difference between psychotic and mystical experiences, and the physiology behind these so called mystical experiences.

But I became particularly interested near the middle of the book, where the author begins to discuss humanism.

After discussing the so called mystical experiences as strictly human experiences, he urges people to acknowledge our common humanity. Here he characteristically expunges god from the equation, because humanism indeed is the goal of his book. He urges people to focus on the humanity that binds us, not the superficialities that divide us. Equipped with this attitude, human beings he suggests will inherit a much more peaceful world.

Dr. K Sohail

But despite his preference for secular philosophies, the author is willing to acknowledge the role of religion in society. In fact, on page 73, he alludes to the relationship between religion and humanism—one that is clearly uncomfortable at times. The author draws a distinction between theo-centric faiths and those more focused on humanity. My own experience also tells me that some religious traditions are more humanistic than others, and more humanistic than theistic.

As part of the religious philosophies of these theocentric faiths, it is righteous to take the lives of other human beings if they fail to subscribe to accepted notions of God. Such an attitude is neither rational nor compassionate. Humanism on the other hand is equated with rationalism and Buddha as the founder of a religious tradition is the perfect rationalist and religious humanist according to the author.

Further along the book, Dr Sohail speaks of God as a metaphor. I am often intrigued by this phrase. And I have often struggled to understand what it means. However, the author's explanations of the phrase are as lucid as his analysis of other complex philosophies and ideas. After reading his explanations, it dawned on me that he confirmed what I thought the phrase meant. Can the idea of a God be seen as a human attempt to objectify all that is good?

Allow me to explain my point. The human world is not as black and white in its experience of good and evil. Good exists in a diluted form. So does evil, even though pessimists may assert that evil is far more unbridled than good. Human beings, however, like to see ideas as absolutes, therefore, good comes to be objectified as God and evil gets objectified as Satan. God, therefore, becomes a metaphor for all that is good. When prophets and sages tell us something is from God, it is immediately accepted as sound and moral without question.

Unfortunately, much that is immoral has been accepted as good over the centuries, simply because it is seen as having emanated from God. It is only now, in the last one hundred years or so, that human beings have been able to de-sanctify religious icons by freeing themselves from the clutches of blind acceptance. And it is part of human evolution, as promoted by Dr Sohail, to critically examine much of what has been handed down to us as good and moral.

After discussing God as a metaphor, Dr Sohail reveals a personal detail about his own journey—one that resulted in his decision to disown God. He says:

"I realized that all my life I had talked to god and he had never answered. After a long monologue and saying goodbye to god, I fell asleep and He left like one old native Indian grandfather who leaves in the middle of the night when it is time to go, and his family never sees him again "

What therefore is the end purpose of all this? Indeed there is a conclusion to be drawn from these philosophical and spiritual meanderings. According to the author, humanism is the answer and it has seven colours. It is the seventh colour of Humanist culture that needs to be instilled in human beings across the world as described in Dr Sohail's own words. He writes:

"It is my dream that we will reach the stage in human evolution where we can see a humanist culture all over the world. I believe that unresolved conflicts of class, gender , race, sexual orientation, language, nationality and religion, continue to be the cause of human suffering and we need to work together to create a just and humanist culture. "

Further down he states:

"We need a critical mass of humanists who are committed and dedicated and willing to work to create humanistic traditions. "

In his earlier chapters, he proposes that religious humanists must be included in this struggle. He has in fact established an avenue for religious people who believe in universal human values, to join hands with secular humanists in this great quest. In his characteristic spirit of accommodation, Dr

Sohail insists that religious people can also accommodate differences and work towards a more equitable world.

Lets see how some organizations and movements across the globe are working to realize this goal and whether according to the author, this critical mass of religious and secular humanists has achieved anything significant towards attaining peace.

1) Belgium, Netherlands and possibly Germany are refusing to accommodate US tactical nuclear weapons on their soil.

2) Japan is holding on to its article 9 prohibiting it from going to war despite US pressure. Costa Rica, Panama and possibly Bolivia are following suit as part of their new constitutions.

3) The UN wants to elevate the right to "peace" as a human right. Despite pressure from the US to oppose such a move.

4) Global security is being redefined in terms of sustainable, collective human security.

5) The highest echelons of governments have adopted programs to instill a culture of peace among citizens.

6) September 21 st is being proposed as an International day of Peace across the world by the federal government of Canada (Alton, 2010).

It seems the individuals who work so diligently for these organizations have repudiated the notion of the inevitability of war. Whether it is the doctrine of armed jihad or Thomas Aquinas' righteous war, or the contemporary doctrine of preemptive strikes, war must be eradicated. Too much is at stake. I applaud Dr Sohail's efforts in doing his share to achieve world peace through his writings and I extend to him my hearty congratulations for his most recent publication: *The next stage of human evolution*.

30. DR KHALID SOHAIL: SPIRITUALISM AS SECULAR HUMANISM
by Ishtiaq Ahmed

In sharp contrast, modern science and the disciplines of psychology and psychiatry in particular, as well as secular philosophy, do not speak of a soul but of the human psyche.

The contemporary centre of enlightened and frank discussion among Pakistanis on highly contentious subjects is most certainly Canada, where it is possible for community radio and television channels to invite experts to express their views freely. One such program is PASSWORD with Dr Baland Iqbal. Recently, Dr Iqbal invited Dr Khalid Sohail, a practicing psychiatrist, author of several books, and accomplished poet and short-story writer, to speak on a topic I believe many subscribing to a secular-rationalist worldview have been intrigued by, a mystifying experience of intense creativity and realization, as if an inner voice is speaking to us. Such moments can be transformative and transcendental and become a new level of consciousness. The question is, are such experiences spiritual in the sense that religions talk about as connecting with divinity, or is there a rational, materialist basis for them?

This was the challenging puzzle that the compere, Dr Iqbal presented to Dr Sohail to solve. Dr Sohail expounded a very interesting thesis. He asserted that the two main religious traditions of the world—the Middle Eastern comprising Judaism, Christianity and Islam, and the eastern tradition centred on the Indian subcontinent consisting of Hinduism, Buddhism and Jainism—hold that body and soul are distinct and separate entities.

Elaborating the Islamic theological standpoint specifically, Dr Sohail said it was premised on the assumption that the soul/souls exists as a non-material entity in a heavenly domain. When a human being is born, one of the souls is placed in that body. After that human being dies his/her soul returns to the same heavenly domain. There the souls wait for the Day of Judgment when each would be held accountable for that person's conduct on earth and then either rewarded with paradise or sent to hell to face punishment. On the other hand, the sub-continental theory is that every human being is born with a soul. However, when that person dies, the soul does not return to some place to wait; rather it keeps returning to earth until it cleanses itself of all sin and then joins the Universal Spirit or God. The ontological distinction drawn by religions is therefore between body and soul as two different entities: one physical, the other spiritual.

In sharp contrast, modern science and the disciplines of psychology and psychiatry in particular, as well as secular philosophy, do not speak of a soul but of the human psyche. It is not separate from the mind or brain; it exists as long as the brain is functioning. It perishes once the brain ceases to function. More importantly, the human brain comprises two chambers that are interconnected. There is a left brain and a right brain. The left brain enables us to reason, calculate, plan and undertake detached thinking while the right brain is about feelings, ethics, morals and compassion. Normally, we use both but one can dominate the other. Dr Sohail mentioned that there was medical evidence that some people who suffered brain injury or have had epileptic experiences spoke of being transported into a different world of fantastic images and voices, which suggested that their right brain had become extra-active.

According to this scientific approach, both religious and secular people experience spirituality as an extra dimension in their lives. While some religious spiritualists become recluses and indulge in excessive meditation, others translate their spiritualism into love of humankind—God, humankind, and creation in general, become one great, indivisible cosmological reality. With regard to the Islamic tradition, Dr Sohail observed that while the *ulema* understand God as power and authority to whom submission is due all the time, the Sufi understands God as love. Consequently, some Sufis embrace all human beings without demanding adherence to any strict dogma. They exude such vibes that people around them experience great peace and comfort. He described Abdus Sattar Edhi and Mother Theresa as religious spiritualists. Equally, secular individuals who consider their lives as part of an undifferentiated humanity and are always at the forefront for the respect of human rights, women's rights, minority rights and even nature rights, and take up cudgels on behalf of the oppressed, are secular spiritualists. Dr Sohail then spelt out the social and political implications, preconditions for both types of spirituality to co-exist and energise one another. He argued that only in a secular-democratic and pluralist social and political order could both exist in harmony.

From a social science perspective, Dr Khalid's thesis is path breaking and needs to be discussed widely. In the interview, he mentions Sigmund Freud, Carl Jung, Karl Marx, Jean Paul Sartre and a host of other thinkers and theorists and elaborates other aspects of these two types of spiritualism. He also proposed a radical new idea: the evolutionary process Charles Darwin discovered, and which was the most revolutionary, transformative theory since Copernicus and Galileo began to question the Biblical theory of the origin of the universe and earth, now needs to be supplemented by an evolutionary theory of thinking. Humankind has to choose between, on the one hand, fanaticism, tribalism, war and continued injustices and, on the other, a world order based on peace, accommodation, adjustment and justice. His two books that I consider essential reading are The Next Stage of Human Evolution, and in Urdu, *Insaani Shaoor ka Irtiqa*. Both are displayed on his website. I warmly recommend that we listen to his interview at http://www.youtube.com/watch?v=V-px_pZPq0c&feature=autoshare

SOURCE:
http://www.dailytimes.com.pk/default.asp?page=2012\12\23\story_23-12-2012_pg3_6

31.   *FAIZ, A POET OF PEACE FROM PAKISTAN*
by Arif Waqar

It's sad that a book comprising some valuable work on Faiz has remained in oblivion for the last two years.

During my recent visit to Canada I had a chance encounter with this book—a collection of articles on the life and times of Faiz Ahmed Faiz.

The first thing that grabbed my attention was the high quality paper, superb printing and an aesthetically designed title page. My first impression was that the book was printed in Canada. But when I thumbed through it, I was amazed to learn it was published in Karachi two years ago, during the Faiz centenary year.

It starts with a conversation between the two compilers of the book, Dr Khalid Sohail and Ashfaq Hussain. Using the well-tested classical method of Socratic dialogue, various questions are asked about the poetry, personality and philosophy of Faiz, following a lively discussion which covers a vast array of literary subjects — right from the poetry of Allama Iqbal down to the short stories of Saadat Hasan Manto.

Dr Khalid Sohail has contributed four articles to the book: 'When Faiz was Imprisoned', 'Faiz, Women and Jealousy', 'Faiz and Fame'; although his most important contribution perhaps is 'Faiz in Search of Freedom'. In this fourth article, he quotes the famous Faiz speech in Moscow while receiving the Lenin Peace Prize.

"...Other than mentally deranged people and criminals, all of us believe that freedom and peace are essential for the progress and evolution of life. These characteristics in life help children and women to smile, crops to grow in fields, and writers and artists to express themselves freely. Freedom is necessary for human beings to live like human beings, and to be able to express their qualities of honesty, bravery, and love for justice..."

Pieces of Faiz's poems in English translation are a real treat in these articles. While a bilingual reader can doubly enjoy it with the original Urdu resonating in the background, a western reader will be enchanted by the sheer content of it. Who can deny, for example, the universal appeal of '*mujh se pehli si*

mohabbat meray mehboob na maang':
Do not ask me
For that past love
When I thought
You alone illuminated
This entire world
And because of you
The sorrows of life
Did not matter
I thought
Your beauty gave permanence
To the colours of spring
And your eyes were
The only stars in the universe
I thought
If I could only make you mine
Destiny would, forever be
In my hands.
Now I know
There are afflictions
Which have nothing to do with desire
Raptures
Which have nothing to do with love.
— *Tr. Daud Kemal*

Translating poetry is tricky. Some insist on defining poetry as a genre that cannot be translated into another language and that can't even be re-phrased in the same language.

It is true that compared to prose, poetry is harder to translate, but it was only through the institution of translation that we were introduced to Greek, Latin, Arabic and Persian poetry.

Incidentally, the book under discussion has two articles on this very subject. Naomi Lazard in his essay, 'Translating Faiz' describes his own method of rendering Faiz into English:

"Faiz gave me the literal translation of a poem. I wrote it down just as he dictated it. Then my real work began. I asked him questions regarding the text. Why did he choose just that phrase, that image, that metaphor? What did it mean to him? What was crystal clear to an Urdu speaking reader meant nothing to an American. I had to know the meaning of every nuance in order to re-create the poem"

Another article on this topic is by Victor Kiernan. This scholarly essay originally appeared as an introduction to 'Poems by Faiz' — published in 1971. Victor Kiernan discusses in detail the origin of Urdu language and its relationship with Persian, Arabic and local Indian dialects:

"When the Mogul empire faded, and with it the old cultural links with Persia, it was chiefly the poetical part of the legacy of Persian that Urdu fell heir to... So much of the spirit and tone of Urdu poetry derives from Persian tradition that this ancestry must often be kept in mind, even when a poet like Faiz is alluding to quite contemporary matters..."

Readers of Faiz know very well that he also wrote excellent prose, both in Urdu and English, but few people know about his Punjabi poetry. A small section at the end of his compiled works 'Nuskha Hae Wafa' contains some Punjabi poems.

Allama Iqbal was once asked why he did not write poetry in his mother tongue, as his contemporary Tagore did. Allama's answer was that he spoke Punjabi at home, but his literary training was in Persian and Urdu, so he could produce poetry only in these languages. When Faiz was asked the same question, his answer was a bit more elaborate:

"I was overtaken by an awesome realisation despite my desire to write in Punjabi, that for one thing I had not mastered Punjabi literature, and for another, based on whatever I had heard, it was hoping against hope to write like Waris Shah."

Making an insightful observation on the relationship of language and life, Faiz says that folk poetry can never be accomplished in Urdu, for Urdu is the language of the polis, not of the village, be it the village in Punjab or around Lucknow — "Urdu is strictly an urban language, I may, if I endeavour, write poetry matching Ghalib's, but never ever the one matching Bulleh Shah."

Referring to these thoughts of Faiz, one of the contributors to the volume, Muhammad Fayyaz writes, "Significant and far-reaching as these observations are, it seems fair to say that the Punjabi poetry of Faiz successfully presents a synthesis of folk and urban concerns vocalised in an elegant manner."

In another article on the same topic, Professor Manzur Hussain seems reluctant to give Faiz any credit for his Punjabi poetry. He says that after the events of 1968, Punjabi had suddenly become fashionable amongst the Punjabi intellectuals, and Urdu poets like Ahmed Nadeem Qasmi and Faiz Ahmed Faiz also jumped on the bandwagon.

Khalid Hasan had a long association with Faiz while they were both in London. The collection includes three articles by Hasan, 'Faiz: A Personal Memoir', 'Faiz on his Boyhood and Youth', and 'Faiz: A Summing Up'.

The foreign contributors include Peter Manuel, Estelle Dryland, Ziyad Abdelfatteh, Mustefa Fersi, Alex La Guma, Rimma Kazakova and Anatoly Sofronov.

The compilers, Dr Khalid Sohail and Ashfaq Hussain, have taken great pains to collect these articles scattered in magazines and periodicals all over the world.

The book, prefaced by Syed Jaffar Ahmed, is certainly a valuable addition to Faiz literature but, sadly, even after two years of its publication, it's lying somewhere in the basement stores of the Pakistan Study Centre, University of Karachi. Some copies may have come out for personal use, but it was never properly distributed or even introduced to the media.

Faiz: His Poetry,
Personality and Philosophy
Editors/Compilers: Dr Khalid Sohail and Ashfaq Hussain
Publisher: Pakistan Study Centre, University of Karachi
Pages: 496
Price: PKR500

Authors / Compilers
Dr Khalid Sohail
A poet, humanist and psychotherapist, he was born in Pakistan in 1952. He received his MBBS from Khyber Medical College and completed his FRCP in Canada in 1982. At present, he runs his own psychiatry clinic in Whitby, Canada. He is the author of more than 60 books including English and Urdu poetry collections, short stories and essays.
Ashfaq Hussain
A poet, critic and essayist, Hussain was born in Pakistan in 1951. He obtained his Master's degree in Urdu Literature in 1974, and migrated to Canada in 1980. His MA dissertation was

on the poetry of Faiz, which was later published as a book. He has written, compiled and edited several books on Faiz since. He is also associated with the Asian Television Network, Canada.

32.   *LOVE LETTERS TO HUMANITY*
by Ziauddin Ahmed

If you have ever phoned Dr. Khalid Sohail and missed him you must surely have heard his telephone machine say ' The dervish has gone out in search of himself, if he is successful he will return your call, and *jab kabhi aatay hain mairay paas aap - main nikal jaata hoon khud ko dhoondnay, (*when you come to visit me, I leave home to find myself).

The search of the dervish is eternal and perpetual, the day he finds himself he will cease to be a dervish, for in constant search is his becoming and the moment he attains his becoming he ceases to become. This is evident in every story of the book and the dervish in Khalid Sohail is continually seeing and observing, always trying to look for and find meaning in everything he comes across.

Khalid Sohail 'dreams of a just and peaceful world' and that is what his book is dedicated to. This may be a utopia but without a dream of utopia dreams would not exist in the first place, and without dreams no thought of struggle for betterment of the self or that of the other would be born and life itself would be meaningless.

Dr. Khalid Sohail is an apprehensive writer and describes his feelings thus:
"I am afraid
The noise of the outside world
Will drown one day
The music inside."
And just out of that fear maybe, he has become a voracious writer, wishing to leave behind a mountain of material for people to handle and ponder upon. Or it may be, as he one day wrote in his diary,
'The more I write, the more I discover myself,
the more I discover myself, the more I share,
the more I share, the more I connect with others in a meaningful way,
the more I connect with others in a meaningful way,
the more I discover the secrets of making creative friends,
the more I discover the secrets of making creative friends,
the more I learn the art of growing together,
the more I learn the art of growing together,

the more I feel optimistic that our tomorrows
-will be more meaningful and productive than our yesterdays.'

This is supported also by his wish not only to write but to,
"write in a language and style that someone with a grade ten education can read and understand'. He further explains his wish to be a writer because as he says ' writers can play a role in human liberation and give people the courage to be free, emotionally as well as socially, politically and culturally".

Dr. Khalid's art of writing is visible both in prose and poetry and runs through a wide spectrum in each of those mediums. In love letters to humanity, he has taken on the role of a story-teller, narrating different types of stories and episodes. He writes stories of both fact and fiction. Stories of love and suffering. Stories of wants and desires, of both those that are fulfilled and those that seek fulfillment.

Dr. Sohail's 'Love letters to Humanity' are a depiction of his self, his emotions and subsequent conditions both subjectively and objectively. One can see his attachment and detachment with both the situations and characters of his stories. The titles of most of the contents of the book are self-explanatory. One gets a gist of the message of the writings by carefully going through the titles alone. Starting with' My' Muse; he writes :

"My muse is a mystery. Her visit is magical and mystical. It is always a pleasant surprise. I never know what will be next source of inspiration. I cannot plan it. I just wait for it..... She can appear as:
- a beautiful sunset
- a child's innocent smile
- a woman's passionate kiss
- a friend's affectionate hug
- a writer's book
- a patient's crisis
- a sad newspaper article or
- an inspiring movie

Sometimes she whispers in my silence or appears in my dream. Her every visit is a good reason to celebrate....."
He is a dreamer who had to run away from his home town because he found that the atmosphere there was too stifling and

that dreamers there were 'hanged', not only for dreaming but also for questioning the reason for it. The question is :
"if dreamers knew
they would be hanged or crucified
why did they share
their dreams with others?...."

He, like everyone else, is in pursuit of the answer.
He tries his hand at love and its ways, and says in 'A Social butterfly':
"I learnt to love
the Soul more than the body
the essence more than the surface ...."

The essence is perhaps more fleeting than the body and it seems it is still eluding him, for his own soul is wandering in search of its mate as this is the gist of any dervish's lifelong quest.

Khalid Sohail fantasizes and dreams. In the short story 'Sacred' his character wakes up one morning to read the holy book but finds that it has vanished from the shelf. She inquires and finds that all the holy scriptures have somehow disappeared from the world. The world leaders hold a conference as to what was to be done. At the end of which it was reconciled that as humanity recovers it might transform this breakdown into a breakthrough and realize that all human beings are part of one human family as they are children of Mother Earth, perhaps getting peace from within and not needing solace from without.

One of the Bio-Fictional Essays in the book is titled 'Peace Clinics'. Here the author proposes the establishment of a Universal Peace Clinic, the aim of which is to try to understand the dynamics of contemporary political violence and then find ways to help people who become involved in this type of militancy. The whole exercise is a very noble idea indeed.

The section of biography has the article 'My Father's Breakdown or Breakthrough' and gives a gist of the authors own background and movement in the change of his own life patterns. The closing sentence says it all..."I sometimes wonder how much my father's condition played a role in my attempts to understand the mysteries of the mind and become a psychiatrist"

In the interview at the closing of the book Dr. Khalid sums up his feelings as a humanist and says:

'As a humanist I have great respect for humanity. I believe that every human child is like a seed that has a unique temperament and potential. For a seed to become a healthy tree and offer wonderful fruits it needs fertile soil, fresh air, humidity and sunshine. Similarly for a child to become a peace-loving healthy adult he needs love and nurturing and discipline. Children that get all the nurturing they need become successful scientists and artists and politicians and doctors and lawyers, and serve their communities. On the other hand, children who are deprived of love or experience neglect and abuse turn into angry and violent adults. Modern psychology, medicine and literature are helping us find ways to become fully human individually and collectively. I dream of a world where all children will have opportunities to express their full potential.'

It is hoped that humanity reads these love letters and grasps their message, and that one more dreamer sees the fulfillment of his lifelong dream and has a peaceful night's sleep.

33.   *LOVE LETTERS TO HUMANITY*
      by Shahid Akhter

The title, Love Letters to Humanity, encapsulates the core message of this anthology of writings by Dr. Khalid Sohail over a period of more than three decades consisting of poetry, stories, essays, translations, biography and an interview.

This selection is a creative examination of human interactions and relationships. However, the book consists of only a sample and would not even come close to representing the vast array of literary and professional writings by the author. Dr. Sohail is a prolific writer with more than twenty books to his credit and still going strong. Through these selected writings the author allows the reader a glimpse into the deep crevices of his mind, the passion of his heart, the richness of his soul, and the generosity of a person driven by his love for humanity.

One unique attribute of Dr. Sohail's personality is his brutal and somewhat risqué and risky honesty. Even at the danger of appearing brazen, he does not hesitate in **saying what he thinks must be said.** He does not shy away from expressing his most intimate feelings. One thought that I feel has never occurred to him is "What will people think?" Readers will find this immensely endearing; at least this reader did.

The common thread running through the entire selection is his unconditional love for humanity, with all its imperfections and convolutions. He elaborates it more academically in the essays and the interview. However, whether he is sharing his father's biography, writing about turtles or women's liberation; religion or humanism; culture or philosophy; this constant driving force can be felt behind all his creativity. He does not care about the price he may have to pay in style or form. For him it is important to stay with the theme and ensuring that the **message gets across** in the way that he wants. In this endeavour he fully succeeds. Readers may disagree with his message but cannot help but admire his sincerity, passion and sense of purpose.

I found his selection of twenty-five poems by far the most representative of this creative montage. The first of which is My Muse, the mythical daughter of Zeus and the poets' inspiring goddess. The poem is an audacious introduction that prepares the reader for the non-traditional style of Dr. Sohail's approach.

He likes the Word, respects it and uses it in ways that can spur aspiring writers and poets. Creative people can relate to the sentiment's directness and simplicity.

My Muse sets the tone for the rest of the anthology. The reader knows right away where the poet is coming from, what drives him, what is important for him, what matters to him and where is he headed. On top of all that, the reader realizes, right off the bat, how distinct and original is his mode of expression.

The author lays his cards on the table by describing how his Muse visits him. His loving description of
"a beautiful sunset;
a child's innocent smile
a woman's passionate kiss
a friend's affectionate hug
a writer's book
a patient's crisis
a newspaper article or
an inspiring movie"
shows the vastness of his canvas and the richness of his inspirational source.

The reason I chose this short poem as his representative poetic creation is because it compacts elements which are present throughout the selection. He takes liberty with the form and is proud of it. Form is not as important to him as the theme and the content. He wants to say what is on his mind and succeeds in articulating it quite eloquently.
He does not care much what literary critics in general and those who consider themselves as know-alls of poetry in particular will say. There is rhyme and rhythm; meter and format; but he uses it where and when he wants it. He definitely refuses to be limited by it. And that is what endears him to his readers.

Dr. Sohail is by no means the first to adapt this form. Poets like Walt Whitman and even Milton dabbled in free verse. What Khalid has done is liberated himself from the confines set and accepted by anyone, even the masters. He defines his own freedom in the poem, Creative Ideas,
"are like birds;
that come to the garden of my mind;
sit on the branch of a tree;
sing a few songs;
and fly away"

Similarly in a five line poem titled Inspirations he shares his creative process:
"Early in the mornings
creative ideas
descend on the pages of my heart the way
dew drops
descend on the petals of flowers"

His poetry tells stories that are deeply rooted in the cultural richness he experienced growing up in the North West Frontier Province of Pakistan. The poem "A Story Teller" could as well have been lifted from the famous Qissa Khawani Bazaar or the Marketplace of Story Telling in Peshawar, the capital city of the Province. The poem takes the reader to ancient scenes of Pashtuns sitting in a circle smoking their water pipes and drinking the delicious qahwa, enthralled by the mesmerizing storyteller. Khalid richly draws on the cultural experiences to make his point.

The poem "Dreamers" similarly expresses his burning passion and the message in his prayer:
"in our ethnic, linguistic and religious rivers
we will all meet
in the ocean of humanity"

Dr. Sohail is fond of sharing his deeply personal and intimate experiences with his readers. His poems like " A Social Butterfly" and "A Human Miracle" would be great material for a Catholic Priest's confessional booth. He has no hesitation in expressing his vulnerabilities and his rebelliousness; his contradictions and his conformities; his human frailties and his character's strength in many other poems including "Now He Radiates Wisdom", "Who Is He", and "Leaving Home".

Khalid has a sense of reality and does not seem to believe in abstractions. He proudly names names where he thinks they should be shared with his readers. In poems like "A Darvesh is Born" "Last Night" and "Kissing Your Tears" he brings the verse to life in real time, in real places and with real people.

In his poems like "Wind, My Companion" and "A New Story" he combines a descriptive, prescriptive and, despite all that goes on in the world, an optimistic approach not only to his muse and to his art but also to life itself.

Through the medium of his poetry, Dr. Sohail forthrightly shares his upbringing in the rough and tumble of the rocky North

West Frontier Province with the reader. His childhood spent in a strict traditional religious environment evolved into a personality that owes a lot to his formative years. It is a mark of creative maturity to accept the deck of cards one has been dealt and then play the best hand with it. The author has made the best of whatever riches or impoverishments; challenges and opportunities; travails or comforts; his early life sent his way.

Although most of his writing shows conscious pulling away from that traditional and religious environment, the more distance he creates from his roots, the more it seems he reveals it through the mystic and spiritual Oneness with Humanity. But he does it in his own inimitable way, safely laying claim, to quote a famous crooner, "I did it my way".

But his "way" also poses some questions purely in literary terms that have nothing to do with the writer's philosophy, convictions or cultural background. In this case one can frankly ask (considering that frankness is a virtue that the author admires most) the following question: Is poetry simply the expression of ideas in non-prose form? If so, then the poetry section of the book is enormously rich. Ideas about hope, love, friendship and justice are expressed with a great deal of passion and force of conviction. However, if poetry means beauty of melody and musicality, metaphor, rhythm and rhyme within the constraints of form and meter, in accordance with the generally accepted rules of poetry, then perhaps prose would have been a better medium for the sentiments expressed in his English poetry.

The author talks about how his writing has kept him honest with himself, and this clearly shows. Often, there is such abundance of honesty that he leaves very little to the imagination as in his poems Waiting; Invisible Chains and My Story. He is so safe in his chosen medium of expression that he does not even bother to cloak his expression in what in the Urdu poetry is known as *Thashbeeh o Istaara*. In his poetry he is very direct and subtlety is rarely attempted.

The stories the author read as a child inspired him to become a writer. He was lucky that he found a receptive audience in his childhood and adolescent friends. Generally children can be very cruel and easily turn their creative companions into laughing stocks but in the author's case his class mates actually found him amusing and thus encouraged him to continue to indulge in his passion of writing. He was able to pursue his dream without running into any major emotional or psychological crisis brought about by others or himself.

He shares with the reader that his therapeutic instincts work wonders through his keeping a personal diary. He transmutes his life full of events, and events full of life, into literary forms of poems, fictions or essays. He calls this anthology an intellectual buffet sharing different forms of his creative expressions and a wide range of encounters with his muse. The collection shows many older tensions, frustrations, struggles, and controversies from early childhood, adolescence, youth, and professional life all meshed into a single dynamic of his love for humanity. On some occasions it feels as if the author is reproducing entries from his intimate personal diary or thinking aloud and jotting down thoughts as they occur to him without any varnish or embellishment.

There has been an ongoing debate in literary circles questioning whether or not literature should have a purpose. In Dr. Sohail's case, and here his vast circle of friends will bear witness to this, love of humanity is the true purpose of all human endeavour, including literature.

As classical Sufi poets used all expression of love, oneness, consummation or separation symbolically for directing the reader or listener to the path of true divine love, in the same way almost all the characters and incidents in the author's short stories and literary work point to love of humanity. He is a twenty-first century Sufi who has rebelled against even the old forms of Sufism, especially Sufism as a mystical dimension of Islam, and created his own path on which he is travelling without fear or concern.

The prose section of the anthology is a potpourri of stories, translations, biography, essays and an interview. As in the poetry segment, the prose also has the overarching theme of his love for humanity. The first story about baby turtles is also representative of his connecting every utterance with his message, aspiration, prayer and primal desire for survival of the species. He is fascinated by turtles. Those of us who have visited him in his office were intrigued by his immense collection of turtles. His is an office turtle galore: rock turtles, clay turtles, wood turtles, paper turtles and metal turtles of all sizes and shapes. Only another psychotherapist, as capable as Dr.

Sohail, can explain the deeper reason for this fascination. But the reader is moved by the struggle of the multitudes of baby turtles for survival. His love for humanity is inseparable from his admonition, appeal and ultimatum to the human species about its indulgence in self-annihilation.

His story "Bigamy" exceptionally conforms to the classical story form. It has a plot, suspense, engaging narration, true to life dialogue and above all, the punch line where Susan congratulates her husband on his "special day" and tells him that her lawyer would be getting in touch with him. The story is also reflective of his vast knowledge of cultural and sociological practices of Pakistanis living in remote areas. It may come as a surprise to many readers that there are areas in Pakistan where a woman can marry more than one husband.

Many readers would wish that all stories had the same engagement but this clash of cultures remains a relative exception in the book. This does not mean that he has not written other stories like that. It is just that they have not been included in this anthology.

The scope of the review does not allow the detail to do justice to most of Dr. Sohail's stories. I want to mention one more which represents his style and message. The story Roots-Branches-Fruits reminded me of a classical movie I had seen way back in the 60s. In the Three Faces of Eve, Joanne Woodward, Paul Newman's wife in real life, plays the role of Eve who has multiple personalities. The depiction of three Eves by Ms. Woodward was a powerful representation of each of the three women. In Dr. Sohail's story, his three brothers, Mohammad, Khalid and Sohail, living in Canada, are shown as having three completely different traits and personalities. I am sure many readers are not aware that Dr. Sohail's full name is Mohammad Khalid Sohail. The story beautifully captures three different aspects of the same person which can be completely different even contradictory on occasions. The masterful weaving of these three characters chronicles show what could be the author's own aspirations, fears, hopes, confusions and reflections. Mohammad is very traditional father of two teenage daughters and is a devout Muslim. On the surface he seems not only dissimilar but also the nemesis of Dr. Sohail. But he also has a lot of what Dr. Sohail had as a child. The author's upbringing had the possibility of turning him into the Mohammad of the story quite easily. The potential was there, only the author's life took a different turn. Khalid, in Roots-Branches-Fruits is a playboy and shares many elements of Dr. Sohail's life. The Sohail character is modern, balanced and perhaps would reflect real Dr. Sohail more closely. But the story goes to show that lifestyle choices are not easy. There are always inner demons that we constantly fight. In the movie Eve comes together. In Khalid Sohail's story the split seems permanent but the love and respect for the difference is also permanent.

Many English writers from India and Pakistan have helped evolve the language. However, there is something else about the usage of English language that gives away the foreignness of the sub-continent's English writers. For example, the use of poetess instead of poet, actress instead of actor and similar examples where South Asian-ness in language becomes very identifiable.

It is by no means a criticism but a compliment to his methodology and self-discipline that Khalid's writing seems contrived. While creative writing is generally believed to be a form of art, there is no denying the fact that it is also a craft. Although he does not mention it in the Anthology, I am privileged to know that he is a very disciplined writer and dedicates scheduled time to the craft of writing. That explains the conscious and deliberate choices of certain words, forms, expressions and style. He balances this deliberation with great skill by never compromising his passion, spontaneity and all-encompassing message.

Khalid has also experimented with Concrete Verse in this anthology. In My Story he seems to have borrowed from the visual format of Lewis Carroll's Alice In Wonderland and, like the famous Mouse's tail, spun a tale about various stages of evolution almost as a sculpted poem. Even if this is done as an architectural poetic experiment, it certainly is an endearing departure from the commonplace.

Considering that most of what Dr. Sohail has written is only partially fictional or purely poetic, his persona of the Dervish interfaces interestingly with the content of his writing. He is not one for false modesty. There are traces of narcissism in his writings, although he is too sophisticated to blow his own trumpet pointing in his own direction. Instead, most of his stories, poems and essays contain autobiographical allusions and it becomes obvious early in the reading as to who is being complimented as liberal, humanist, open minded, democratic and creative.

This anthology does not fit in any mold. It is an interesting experience to read so much variety in one volume. I would have liked reading separate anthologies of his poetry, fiction and essays. But then one would be deprived of the pleasure of sampling within one volume the wide-ranging smorgasbord of a very distinct writer who refuses to be stereotyped just to make life easy for the critic.

To gain an adequate comprehension of the anthology it is essential that it be read in its entirety. Reading it just in parts does not give the reader the true feel of exhaustiveness of Khalid's approach. He is a lover of such insatiable intensity and broadness that he wants to embrace and love entire humanity, not just segments of it. If the reader leaves the book with an enhanced appreciation of human suffering, aspirations, fears and dreams, then Dr. Sohail's efforts will have served their purpose.

Khalid's whole life revolves around his passion for humanity. His lifestyle, his friendships, his appearance, his inseparable satchel of manuscripts that he always carries with him, and his very passionate romantic life, all that and much more shows a candidness, warmth and friendliness that is driven by love in all its manifestations.

Dr. Sohail does not claim to possess the panacea for all evils facing humanity. He may not offer the methodology for its cure. That is not his role. However, he does encourage readers to make whatever contribution they can to ensure the world is a better place because of them. His love letters certainly inspire the reader to have a new respect, a new fondness and above all a new sense of responsibility towards humanity. He stimulates us into doing our part to make sure that our love for humanity acts as a bond to bring all the inhabitants of this planet together regardless of their tribe, race, colour and creed.

It is hard for me to separate the man from the poet and the writer. His personality gleams through his words in the anthology. It is quite possible that a harsh critic's microscopic search may find some technical format shortcomings. But I feel Khalid makes up for these misgivings so that the overall impact of this book leaves the reader with a great deal of admiration for the author, a new respect for the planet and a fresh appreciation for the role each one of us can play as an important member of the human race.

Note: *Love Letters to Humanity* is published by Sang-e-Meel Publications 25, Shahrah-e-Pakistan [Lower Mall] Lahore Pakistan 2013

34.   A BROKEN MAN
by Ikram Brelvi

I need not elaborate on what is fiction and who is Khalid Sohail as both are well known to those who take even little interest in Urdu literature. In short, Khalid Sohail is a poet, a short story writer, a psychiatrist by profession and passion, and a young man of strong conviction, a very amiable person and, above all, a paean of humanity. Fiction has come naturally to him; and as you all know, the 'chief function', according to Henry James, 'is to entertain, to be interesting; but it often serves to instruct, to edify, to educate, to persuade and to arouse a sense of the sublime'. It is also one of the literary devices by which a writer communicates his vision and philosophy and the nature of reality in concrete terms. The concrete forms of fiction are:

A.   Novel
B.   Short Story
C.   Drama or narrative poem
D.   Novella and
E.   Novelette

Here, in this modest essay, I am concerned with the novelette. To repeat the cliché, Khalid Sohail and fiction are both happily wedded and are well known to the lovers of literature for their popularity.

To start, '*de novo*', during the hundred years, traditional philosophies reeled under the impact of scientists like Darwin, Pavlov and Freud. Bertrand Russel contributed to the intellectual, political and moral turmoil. Karl Marx added to the turbulence. The ideals of these professional scientists and philosophers were translated and conveyed to reflective readers by giant playwrights and novelists: Ibsen, Strinberg and, of course, George Bernard Shaw, and some lesser giants like John Galsworthy and H. G. Wells, and still later, writers like Aldous Huxley and George Orwell.

Few have succeeded in integrating psychoanalysis into the main traditional systems of theory concerning the human mind and its interaction with human behaviour as in 'A Broken Man', wherein a true picture of the problems of an Asian immigrant have been so vividly projected in novelette form. 'In

Two Boats', a short story included in this book, the whole warp and web is interwoven around Asian immigrants who swing in and out of two different cultures, while 'Open and Closed Doors' has its own charm in the mystical rendering with soft surrealistic undertones. 'Devta' is symbolic in nature, aimed at breaking the primordial myth of the 'divine right' of the 'selected few' over the masses. It is, by and large, a refined satire and a drastic reappraisal of the glorification of man, reassuring his place in the social word.

However brief, this creative work of art is significant for its contribution to literature in that it re-orients mankind to ethical dilemmas distinctive of the twentieth century immigrant who migrates from a South Asian country to Canada. Together, the novelette and the three short stories delight us with an impression; an impression that has undercurrents of iconoclasm which induces uncertainty and skepticism towards traditional dogma and religion, rites and rituals as well as written and unwritten moral codes. All the same, such thinking and behaviour lands people like Shahzad and Julie prisoners of conscience and misfortune because they do not conform to the traditional creeds and moral concepts brought to them by their ancestors. And this, throughout the novelette, becomes the motivational force of interaction between the "real ego" and ideal ego' which continues to reflect to a large measure man's relations to his environment and the social world. In this way symbolic distortion caused by deep-rooted inhibitions ingrained in the psyche of Shahzad as a result of parental guidance, make him sadomasochistic and neurotic.

One can also discern traces of cyclothymia in him. This is perhaps a result of being scorned, laughed at and reproached by his elders, especially his father, and the restrictive attitude and authoritative behaviour of the staff of the psychiatric hospital which in Shahzad's eyes was 'no better than a prison cell'. Chapter three of the novelette is very meaningful in that it gives an account of different types of various stages of the psychiatric hospital, for example the bubble room; strange shape, old uses and abuses. This chapter is full of philosophy, meaning of life and ethnic study. All this appears to me symbolic in its nature, and looks like inherent satire on people who command and those who are commanded. The chapter ends beautifully on a pithy note of love for Julie, a passionate redeemer and sympathizer of Shahzad among the staff of the psychiatric hospital.

The mental reflexes and complexes in the novelette provide a new dimension as it was not until the first three or four decades of the twentieth century that creative writers became interested in exploring man's consciousness rather than merely narration of his deeds. Personality and emotions, though psychologically complex, play an important role and are movingly significant in 'A Broken Man'. Shahzad's conditioned reflexes or, to be more appropriate, his militant behaviourism bear testimony to this. Khalid Sohail, in this modest piece of fiction, appears to be interested in abnormal psychology with its important implications for the theoretically normal man. He has, like Marcel Proust and Andre Gide, thrown light on the incongruous elements of personality. He also emphasizes the environmental influences on consciousness and personality, more specifically and demonstrably the influence of Shahzad very skillfully. One wonders whether a web so finely woven could hold such passion and refinement in point of view and whether the delicacy of analysis could encompass the fullness of a major experience. Despite the intellectual raiment, Shahzad is still poor, naked and a speared animal at certain crucial moments, as intellect alone does not project the meanderings of his consciousness and hidden sources of his behaviour.

The fall of Shahzad, as seen in the novelette, is attributable to the fact that he lived up to the command of the 'ego-ideal' which gives rise to a sense of disillusionment, despondency, frustration, guilt and an inferiority complex. This ends up in both internal and external conflict and self-dissatisfaction. That is why he feels comfortable with his doctor and redeemer. Ultimately, the birth of his son, Adam, is the metamorphosis of Shahzad from a sub-human to a human level; prior to chapter six, he appears melancholic, at times manic and then he gradually recovers and becomes closer to normal in his behaviour and attitude. Here, specifically, we see a confrontation with the 'real ego' and the 'ideal ego' for which he suffers extreme depression. He often accuses himself of many unpardonable crimes while his conscience is echoed in the form of hallucinated words of reproach and remorse:

'I am a thief, a gambler, a drunkard, and a fornicator. I even have a bad record with the police. For quite some time I have been involved in selling cocaine and amphetamines. I am fed up with life; the whole thing is a tragic play'

'I am a criminal, a sinner and a black sheep in the eyes of other people and a culprit as far as the law was concerned'.

In the words of Margarethe Von Andics, 'the knowledge of having some definite responsibility or of doing some work of importance is a potent safeguard against the temptation to take one's own life'. Shahzad, who was at the verge of committing suicide prior to the birth of his son, changed as soon as the idea of raising Adam came to his mind following the death of Julie who was discredited by the Board of Doctors.

The re-entry of a criminal, Shahzad, into an all-embracing human common experience is achieved through the co-operation and timely support of Abraham. The influence of Abraham over Shahzad is nicely interwoven despite his entering very late in the novelette. The older, wiser gentleman undoubtedly plays a vital role in changing the life pattern and thinking of Shahzad. The Jewish story about the differences between heaven and hell is very pertinent, and, at the conclusion of the story, the remarks of Abraham are highly aphoristic:

'No one can change another person's life. We all have the same beginning and end.'

Now, a few words about the novelette, a work of prose fiction of intermediate length, longer than a short story and shorter than a novel, since there is little agreement on the maximum length for any of these types the distinction is that, in general, the novelette displays the customary compact structure of a short story with the addition of greater character development, theme and action. Congruent with this, Khalid

Sohail's 'A Broken Man' is in itself nicely interwoven like Herman Melville's 'Billy Budd', R.L. Stevenson's 'Dr. Jekyll and Mr. Hyde', Henry James' 'The Turn of the Screw', Joseph Conrad's 'Heart of Darkness', Turgenev's 'On the eve', Guy d'Maupassant's 'Odyssey of a Prostitute', Tolstoy's 'The Death of Ivan Ilych', Ernest Hemingway's 'The Old Man in the Sea' and Gabriel García Márquez' 'Innocent Erendira', and so forth.

Taking into account the complexity of character portrayal and action, I feel that "A Broken Man" demands a wider canvas. Notwithstanding this, in its present shape, it is a perceptive work of art and makes an interesting study of the intricate problems faced by immigrants coming to Canada from an entirely different set of beliefs and cultures. The novelette beautifully mirrors the decay and divergences and also establishes adequately that 'A Broken Man' is a woeful story of a man who was 'split apart', he has struggled all of his life against the influence of his parents, relatives, friends, even his love for God. He fell prey to the police and again landed in the psychiatric hospital from where he had earlier managed to escape.

Apart from the main character of Shahzad, small characters like Cathy, the disabled woman, Derek, the drug peddler and crooked friend of Shahzad, Saleem, Christine, Cynthia, Julie, Abraham, Rachel and even Adam have been drawn with passionate care and concern. Khalid Sohail ascribes to the philosophy of Henry James in writing fiction, that:
'Catching the very note and trick, the strange irregular rhythm of life, that is the attempt whose strenuous force keeps Fiction upon her feet'.

This is precisely what Khalid Sohail has adhered to in his novelette, to intensify the effect and catch the classic rhythm and grace.

35. FROM HOLY WAR TO GLOBAL PEACE
by Farzana Hassan, 2014

Dr Khalid Sohail's book, *From Holy War to Global Peace* published by Multiline Publications Lahore, is a timely and effective address of much of the politics of the world today. It includes an incisive commentary on the various militant movements of the twentieth and early twenty-first century, while offering pragmatic solutions to the ideological belligerence that plagues contemporary international politics. The first chapter also includes a candid account of the author's journey from being a religious devotee ready to wage a jihad, to becoming a citizen of the world in every true sense of the word. In other words, the author presents a heartfelt rationale as to why a narrow and myopic view of the world engendered by religious zeal must be abandoned in favour of a more humanistic and universalistic relationship to one's fellow human beings.

We are painfully aware of the dramatic turn of events in countries like Syria and Iraq, where the most pernicious Islamist forces are waging a jihad against states, governments and even ordinary citizens. They are pursuing an apocalyptic agenda that desires a global caliphate shaped in its entirety by the most obscurantist and vicious brand of sharia law. Such a worldview engenders hostility toward all who profess a different understanding of the world, and works to annihilate everything that stands in its way. Even Muslims who are seen as deviating from God's chosen path have suffered the brutality that has become commonplace in ISIS controlled areas. These political developments are exceedingly dangerous, as ISIS militants wish to fulfil an apocalyptic vision. They will not give up their jihad until they see their end-time scenarios realized, as they believe in the absolute moral validity of their movement. It is an ideology inspired by an understanding of Islam that is supported by both religious texts and historical precedent, therefore its proponents function with a degree of religious authority that is perhaps missing from other expressions of Islam as a lived faith.

Dr Sohail has done well to provide readers with an analysis of the roots of this modern day jihadism. He delves into the writings of ideologues like Syed Qutb in the chapter entitled

"Syed Qutb, a Leader of Muslim fundamentalists". He discusses Qutb's fundamentalist approach to matters of faith, coupled with his abhorrence of Western culture, institutions and politics. The author also points out that Qutb despised communism as well. It is Qutb's book, *Milestones*, that has inspired a whole new generation of Muslim jihadists of the late twentieth and early twenty-first century. He shows how Qutb assumed the mantle of Hassan Al Banna, the founder of the radical and militant Muslim Brotherhood established in Egypt. It is the philosophies of Islamist writers like Qutb and Al-Banna that have shaped the tenets of modern Islamism and jihadism. It includes the following characteristics that the author identifies from a social, political and most importantly, psychological standpoint.

Islamists of today have developed an acute sense of Muslim identity that transcends the bounds of region, race, nationality, linguistic or cultural differences. Islamists believe in a pan Islamist worldview where the entire world will have to be subjugated, so that Islam is established, at least politically, all across the world. They are willing to fight toward this end, obliterating anything and everything that stands in their way. For this, they may employ all the tactics of guerilla warfare, that in the contemporary religio-political climate has acquired a more lethal character in the form of terrorism. Dr Sohail also professes the view that the Muslim world is irate due to what it perceives as Western expansionism. There is also the unresolved conflict in the Middle East that continues to take lives and wreak destruction on innocent populations. Dr Sohail also notes that this sense of a primary identity is common to all guerilla fighters.

He narrates the biographies of many such "freedom fighters" and guerilla warriors in the second half of the book. In this section he includes the biographies of Manachem Begin, Nelson Mandela, Che Guevara and Mao Zedung, all individuals who played a pivotal role in the makings of twentieth century politics. He tries to find a common thread in these movements, suggesting that all of these individuals were cause-driven people, passionate enough to even pay the ultimate price for their cause. However, in providing a panoramic view of these various twentieth century guerilla movements, Dr Sohail has also provided for us an opportunity to examine the stark contrast they represent against contemporary Islamist movements.

While the struggles of Nelson Mandela and Mao Zedung

were directed towards certain political ends, their armed struggles came to a halt once those ends were achieved. The Islamists on the other hand believe in jihad as an integral part of Islam that must be pursued on an ongoing basis. They also believe in end time scenarios and therefore pursue their objectives with an apocalyptic zeal that represents a fundamental difference between jihadism and the politically inspired movements of the twentieth century. These can easily be perceived as self-limiting struggles that ended with the objective being reached. Islamists see their struggle as far more protracted. Furthermore, any movement that embodies within itself the authority of religion, always tends to be far more virile in how it formulates and executes its agenda. Islamists believe they are fighting for God, to establish God's rule. They feel that their efforts have been provided validation by the Quran and the Sunnah of the Prophet Muhammad. Religious fighters are also far less amenable to entertaining counter arguments against their cause, once again, because they feel they must take their guidance from religious texts they consider divinely inspired and irrefutable.

The most important part of the book in my humble view is the one that deals with peacemaking efforts. The bio-fictional essay shared by the author must be disseminated far and wide. It speaks volumes about the efforts some individuals have made throughout the course of history, especially in the twentieth century. What peace-making requires is an acute sense of justice, an unflinching commitment to peacemaking, a sharp capability to forestall any impediments to the process, and an overall universalistic and humanistic worldview that recognizes no distinctions of race, creed or colour.

Dr Sohail points out that peace must be built within all strata of society. Peace must be economic, political, social and religious. Individuals who hold divergent views in a particular community must still be able to uphold such opinions without fear of retribution. In pointing out the various types of peace, Dr Sohail has highlighted a very important building block toward a wholesome society. Dr Sohail says that some peacemakers like Kofi Annan were at times able to achieve political peace, but fell short of eliminating the tensions that often fester in a society at the social and economic level.

As a psychiatrist, Dr Sohail also lists some important

facts about modern day jihadists. He states that they belong mostly to the Wahabi and Salafi sects of Islam. Many are followers of Syed Qutb and Maududi, and have been brainwashed by contemporary cult leaders. He also points out that militants belong to all faiths and can be Hindu, Christian or Buddhist. He says that in his clinical study he discovered that these militants not only subscribed to a fundamentalist ideology, they also had fundamentalist personalities, in that they only regarded their own philosophy as the ultimate truth. In developing these personalities, they were frequently influenced by family and community. These are all valuable insights that must be included in any program to prevent radicalization.

The following practical steps can also be taken to de-radicalize militants according to the author. These include, isolating the militant from his group to prevent continued negative influences, introducing better religious discourse, getting radicals to "meet the enemy" so they know the enemy is just as human, helping them to come to terms with their own grief, educating them about political conflicts, developing a strong peace consciousness, developing critical thinking and developing creativity.

These are all practical suggestions that can use by therapists across the world in attempting to create a more peaceful society. The book is a must-read for all who wish to understand the mechanics of modern warfare, which tends to be asymmetrical due to terrorism and guerrilla warfare. The solutions in the book must also be widely shared, as they provide hope for peace to prevail in a much troubled world.

36.   *DR. SOHAIL'S RELENTLESS SEARCH FOR PEACE*
by Dr. Sehdev Kumar

Dr. Khalid Sohail's book, *From Holy War to Global Peace*, is a collection of deeply-felt reflections on suicide bombers, guerrilla warriors and peacemakers. As a young man growing up in Pakistan in 1960s, Dr. Sohail tells us, that he could have easily turned into a suicide bomber. Such was the messianic appeal of the religious and nationalistic hate-mongers that any impressionable youth could be so suckered into frenzy and destruction.

Fortunately for Dr. Sohail, and for all of us who seek and yearn for humane solutions to the social inequities and injustices, he saw a different light and chose a different path – a path of peace and persuasion.

In this engaging book, the author—a well-known psychotherapist in Toronto—traces the psycho-social dynamics of fanatic religious forces that operate on the young and the gullible in Pakistan, Iraq, Palestine, Afghanistan and elsewhere, and how they wreak destruction on one and all. How can they, Dr. Sohail asks again and again with heart-rending poignancy, unleash such devastation in the name of a God that is supposed to be merciful and forgiving? How has such a God been created and by whom, he wonders.

Dr. Sohail's commitment is to life and to its celebration in all its rich fecundity; honoured as 'Humanist of the Year' in Toronto in 2006, as a poet and a healer, he is ardently drawn to serve one and all. He rejoices in the messages of the Sufis and their celebration of oneness of all beings. He is touched by the grandeur of the songs of Kabir and the wisdom of Krishnamurti. Whosoever sings of the wonders of life, is his friend and a fellow-traveller. Anyone who impedes the flow of life, whatever their religious or ideological pretensions, is not for him.

Suicide bombers have been centre-stage for some time now among several Muslim countries. Their origin, however, can be traced back at least to the young Kamikaze warriors in Japan in 1940; they were not driven by religion but by fanatic nationalism, in which the emperor himself was divine. Such nationalistic fervour was to inspire the Tamil Tiger suicide bombers. Here, in this book, Dr. Sohail traces the history of encounter between fundamentalist Islam and secular forces in

Egypt, and how they were often manipulated and exploited by America as part of its cold war strategy. The political and religious developments in Saudi Arabia, Iraq, Egypt, Palestine and Pakistan are very much intertwined with 'God-less' Soviet Union and the Christian fundamentalists of USA.

This is how Dr. Sohail explores briefly the various guerrilla movements under the leadership of Mao in China, Ho-Chi Minh in Vietnam, Che Guevara in South America, Nelson Mandala in South Africa. What were such charismatic leaders driven by? By the hatred of the enemy or by the love for the oppressed? Dr. Sohail is sympathetic to their concerns, but still he wonders if good ends can justify violent means?

From these revolutionaries, Dr. Sohail moves on to comment on the peacemakers: Mandala proves to be peacemaker in a 'Rainbow Nation' with his right-hand man Archbishop Tutu; Gandhi struggles peacefully for India's independence and no less for the transformation of his own society, so riven by social and religious inequities, and then to be assassinated by a zealous Hindu; Abdul Ghaffar Khan in Pakistan – known as 'Frontier Gandhi' – is steadfast to the end in his secular, humanistic vision.

Working as a psychotherapist in post-911 Toronto, with endless incidences of Muslim fanaticism on one hand and Islamophobia on the other, Dr. Sohail's commitment to secular humanism played itself out by the creation of 'Peace Clinics' in many cities where all prejudice and hatred – of many stripes and by many different bearers – could be addressed peacefully and humanely. It is no mean undertaking, for peace cannot be created, whether at home, or amongst communities and nations, unless we are all committed to peace, whether we are in the White House, or in a pulpit in a church or in a mosque, or in a classroom.

Dr. Sohail's goals are worthy; his persuasions are courteous and peaceful; his commitments strike one as unwavering.

It is not without significance that *'From Holy War to Global Peace'* should be published in 2014, on the 100th anniversary of the beginning of the most gruesome war in the human history, fought between the most 'civilized' and scientifically advanced nations of the world.

Well, 'civilization' is a good idea but it needs to be continually nurtured by good people who love life more than their religion or their ideology, and who celebrate creation, wherever and whatever the Creator may be.

Many centuries ago, in 411 BC, a Greek play, *Lysistrata*, addressed this ongoing struggle between the glories of life and the hideous heroism of war. The women in the play go on a sex strike against their warring men; no physical intimacies so long the men continued to indulge in the war. The protest proved to be successful; it seemed, at least in the play, that men had the sense, however briefly, to choose to make love rather than war.

I doubt very much if Dr. Sohail uses any such strategies to propagate peace in his Peace Clinics. However, he does use the word 'psyche' throughout the book. Psyche is a Greek word and a goddess; she encompasses everything: mind, consciousness, the unconscious, spirit, soul. And she finds her full blossoming when touched by Cupid, the god of love.

I wonder if the 72 *houries* that some of the suicide bombers are promised in the afterlife could dissuade them from mayhem and destruction if they were to present themselves to these innocent young men here on earth.

You see, one must Give Peace a Chance!

Dr. Sehdev Kumar is Professor Emeritus at the University of Waterloo. Bioethicist, and historian and philosopher of science, he lectures on Science-Religion Dialogue at the University of Toronto. Author of several books, including *The Vision of Kabir*, his forthcoming book is, *7000 Million Degrees of Freedom*.

37. THE MAN FATE BROUGHT BACK
by Syed Haider

It is hard to find a book which contains so much drama and so many twists and turns. I was really struck by the unusualness of incidents described in this book. Let's look at a few examples. There was a ship which was proclaimed to be unsinkable but tragically it sinks on its maiden voyage, very close to Canadian shores. Then there was a Canadian, from the Lindsay area, who was supposed to sail on this ship but only a few hours before sailing, and supposedly dying, he went out to have just one more drink, one more street fight before hitting the water, he missed the boat and lived happily ever after. As if these twists were not enough, you will find in this book a story of two lovers who went to their graves without knowing the fate of each other. One could not celebrate the miraculous survival of her beloved; the other could not mourn the early death of his lover. These are no fictional happenings; all of these incidents are based on well documented facts. Most of the record of this story would have been lost, if fate did not save a bagful of letters lying under thousands of feet of corrosive ocean water. As a last twist the fate withheld the discovery of that bag until the death of its owner, thus denying him the pleasure of its recovery by just few years. Yes, once in a while fate gets tired of boring routine and surprises us with what it is capable of and how helpless and ignorant about the future we can be.

Although we know we cannot predict the future, when we see unique or exceptional traits in a child or a young man we speculate about what lies ahead for this unusual person and what kind of man this person will become. Even the hero of this book, Howard Irvin, speculated in a poem about his nephew, Claude, one of the authors of this book. These speculations grow even more poignant when one dies early. I am sure in the case of adventurous Howard Irwin, his parents and relatives must have speculated similarly, more so after learning that he perished with the Titanic, wondering what kind of person Howard would have been after visiting 28 US states, sailing seven seas including the Pacific Ocean, visiting five continents including Australia, New Zealand, acquainted with three revolutions and three major revolutionaries—Gandhi, Dr. San Yat San and

Lenin, etc. etc. Fate responded to these speculations and said OK, I will make a rare exception. I will bring back the accomplished Howard Irvin from the dead and I will show you what kind OF person he was destined to be. This book shows us, through Mr. Howard Irvin's own letters and other documents, what kind of man this tough lad from Lindsay became whom the Titanic left behind.

Tough lad Howard was, with limited skills. Working as a tradesman and ship-hand he eked out a meagre living but still was able to travel far and wide and managed to meet so many dignitaries and got involved in some historical movements which is another intriguing part of this book. Let's see what kind of person Howard Irwin turned out to be. Dr. Sohail has very skilfully summarized an answer in this book. He was a creative writer with a wonderful sense of humour. A logical, rational and philosophical man who considered the world of spirits and superstition a realm of stupidity. His desire to be cremated showed his extreme non-religious nature. But like all of us, he had regrets. In his article *Wail* he writes, "The necessities of life for self and others cut short my education in 1900 at the age of twelve. Since then all I have been successful in, is growing old." Howard Irwin then surrenders to the fate by acknowledging that it is natural and peculiar to life itself. Yes, the same fate which saved Howard Irvin from perishing at sea showed us that regardless how much you travel, how many great people you meet, how wise, witty, logical, rational and liberal you become, if 'the necessities of life' overpower you sometimes all that's left is to keep growing old. Still, 'thou shalt not totally surrender to the necessities of life' is a big lesson for all of us. Remember, our only limitations are those we set up in our own minds or permit others to establish for us.

But is it really true in case of Howard Irvin? In my view the answer is emphatically 'no'. It is true that he did not achieve a celebrity status of which he had all the potential. Although he died as a factory worker he will be admired for his thoughts and writings. He definitely added his bit in the repository of human knowledge and wisdom. No doubt, his article *The Last Will* is a masterpiece. But other articles too are no less interesting. In his article on Catherine the Great, Howard Irvin has told stories of earlier immigrants of this land, the hardship they suffered, and the rivalries they faced in establishing themselves in Canada. As

Dr. K Sohail

a new immigrant myself I find these stories fascinating and otherworldly.

It will take a long time if I comment on each and every item of this book especially the letters. I am not sure about the morality of reading someone's private letters, especially love letters. I admit to have read them but before reading I categorized them as research material.

In the end, I want to congratulate the two authors of this book, Dr. Khalid Sohail and Claude Irvin, who conspired with fate and, one more time, brought Howard Irvin back from the dead by publishing this book. Thank you.

38. *MY JOURNEY OF 30 YEARS WITH SOHAIL*
by Anne Henderson, FOTH, December 15, 2013

Thank-you for having me here today to share a unique perspective on Sohail and his writing. You all know he is a psychiatrist and a writer; I have worked with him as a psychiatric nurse and a writer. You hear the stories and see the finished products; I know the backstories and have, one way or another, been part of most of those finished products. It's not possible to give a chronological retrospective of my collaboration with Sohail, as the many parts are interwoven, but I am pleased to offer some highlights of creative Sohail that no-one else can share.

Before I focus on our gathering to honour Sohail, I would like us to remember what else happened today, halfway around the world. They are laying to rest Nelson Mandela, a great fighter for his people's freedom. Sohail and I share a history about Mandela. When my children were small, I used to sit at my kitchen table writing letters as a member of Amnesty International, asking for Mandela's release from prison. He was a young man then. During my years with Sohail, we would discuss Mandela; Sohail used to read Mandela's writings and he was one of those who understood, like Mandela, that there is no peace without justice, and justice often requires struggle, sometimes violent struggle, as those with power and control don't easily give it up. The world acknowledged that when it honoured Mandela over the years, and today the world is saying goodbye to one of Sohail's heroes.

Back here to Sohail. I worked for 40 years as a nurse, mostly in psychiatry. I met Sohail at Whitby Psychiatric Hospital, where I worked as a community mental health nurse attached to an acute admitting unit.

Our first meeting was in 1984. I had visited a patient on a leave of absence at his home. I remember him well, because as we sat on his couch, he pulled out from under it a stick of dynamite. He meant no harm—it was from his days working in construction, but it made for a few tense moments for me. A few days later I was called to a team meeting of Sohail's unit from which the patient had been on his leave. He had drunk alcohol and the staff wanted to discharge him from treatment as drinking was prohibited. Sohail, as the attending psychiatrist, was strong in his advocacy on the patient's behalf; he felt that he should not be discharged from the treatment program. Staff are usually punitive and rule-bound, and doctors are mostly conservative and traditional—not given to overlooking bad behaviour. I still remember looking at Sohail as he walked away—in those days he wore a suit and on this day he had on a dark suit with his short dark curly hair just touching the collar. I am not at all intuitive but thought: here is a man who will change things around here.

Sohail was instrumental in the reorganization of the Outpatient and Admitting departments in the fall of 1984, so that people seeking help would have better care coming into hospital and after they left. Sohail did home visits to see where people lived and how things were in their homes or boarding homes—no other doctor concerned himself with that. He started doing psychotherapy, relationship, and family work; previously staff met with family only to discuss things like placement, education, med compliance). He was frequently in conflict with the unit director regarding more humane approaches and more family-centred care and with other agencies who were too rule-bound and traditional. He was different in those days… played practical jokes, flirted with older ladies from Administration who ventured over to our department—never maliciously but just having fun. They were flattered but unsure how to take him. He was kind to anyone who worked hard for patients' wellbeing, but could be hard on anyone who did not.

I became aware of him as a writer when he published his first Canadian book of short stories, *Breaking the Chains*. He struggled at that time with English as he was not used to writing in it but he persevered. I remember I gave him a dozen red roses which I thought was an elegant gift for a writer. His short stories reflected his compassion as a doctor—themes of loneliness, alienation, need to respect and nurture each other and the earth. He once got into trouble when a copy of a short story was found lying around in the office, as it was critical of women; people apologized when they learned that I had written it. He learned from that the hazards of being a male writer writing anything critical of women in those strongly feminist days.

In 1995, we left the hospital to start a clinic. At my suggestion we called it the Creative Psychotherapy Clinic because he already had a publishing company called Creative

Links. That clinic in itself was creative—nowhere in Canada is there a clinic like that one. We did individual, marital, family and group work, which you will not find anywhere else in Canada in that format. It is a unique approach because of the financial sacrifice that Sohail was willing to make for the comprehensive treatment of his patients, and because of the trust he placed in me to work with him in that way. It was creative for me learning to work closely with Sohail both professionally and in his literary projects, and because I had to learn how to manage an office on day one with no experience. We grew together in our ability to work effectively with people in our care using our contrasting personalities and styles but always united in our goals of restoring people to the best they could be. I was there with him till 2005 and now Bette Davis has taken my place there.

The clinic is creative for his patients in that Sohail encourages his patients to write and indeed to produce any form of art that they can—painting or sculpture, in order to share their experiences, feelings and dreams. Many find that in doing so, they discover talents that had lain sleeping all their lives. Or they knew they had talent but never developed it. He supports people not only to heal, but to discover their special gifts, so that they focus not on the symptoms of their illness, but on their uniqueness as human beings.

During those years, Sohail became interested in making documentaries about mental health issues, and he used to ask his patients to share their stories. That was one thing he and I had creative arguments about...I never supported that because of my concern that they would do it out of affection for Sohail and then regret having their faces and stories out there in public forever. Over the years he was proved right—people like being in the media and we never had any problems doing it. I learned that people felt proud to share their journey with Sohail to healing and personal growth, and it gave them a chance to participate in something exciting and creative. It was also their gift to others.

OTHER AREAS OF CREATIVITY
Creative lunches:

Sohail felt that the lunch break was an important feature of the day. Not just a break from work, squeezed into a short time watching the clock, but an opportunity for renewal and exploration of ideas. Meeting at specific restaurants for lunch, meals would start benignly with an innocent remark by somebody, which led immediately to heated debates—the heat supplied by Sohail. He called it play-fighting. People went back to work after lunch humiliated, vowing never to come for lunch with Sohail again, but of course came right back the next day so they wouldn't miss the next invigorating discussion. There was always the hope that somebody, someday, would prove Sohail wrong. Never happened but we tried for years. These play-fights often provided material for his next essay. We debated everything—politics, ethics, religion, parenting, fashion, patient care, even attitudes towards animals. It was a question Sohail threw out one day and the ensuing discussion, that sowed the seeds years later, of my ceasing to eat any kind of living creature.

Green Zone Philosophy:
    I was there at the beginning when he started using the traffic light analogy to help people understand calm moods and situations, tense moods and situations, and moods and situations that were out of control. Out of those early days of developing and expanding that idea grew numerous books, an entire website, and lectures and presentations.
    He went to Pakistan to interview Javed Iqbal, accused of murdering 100 children. As a psychiatrist he was interested in the person and the motivations, and as the humanist, in fair process. The judge's remarks about having Javed Iqbal's body cut up into 100 pieces and put into a vat of acid were horribly extreme. Sohail's interviews of Javaid Iqbal in his prison cell, his family, and people in the justice system resulted in the book, *The Myth of the Chosen One*, an exploration of the life of Javed Iqbal and the concepts of psychopaths, cults and charismatic leaders. Sohail the psychiatrist and humanist highlighted the man, the justice system and the wider world of personalities like Javed Iqbal, while Sohail the writer brought all those elements together in a fascinating book,
    He never stops thinking, creating, writing. Every encounter is an opportunity for the generation of ideas and constructs. A passing glance at a flower inspires a poem; a discussion over lunch finds an outlet in a letter about the issue. He cannot not write.

His profession provides boundless material for his writings—he might be a poet at heart but he sees patterns and sets in the material he receives. He might love Mother Earth in the abstract, but he is a keen observer of politics around the world, and writes constantly about the struggles of nations and communities.

He mentors other poets, writers and playwrights. I have worked alongside Sohail all these years, as he perfected his style and discussing the content of his many books, poems, essays and articles. In the past few years he has asked me to collaborate with other authors, and in so doing I have encountered other talented and creative people. This work has allowed me with my very modest skills to partake in the creativity of others.

We have been creative partners on this journey, growing together in our language skills, and learning together about the world of publishing, audio and visual media and distribution channels.

I remember saying to a nurse who worked with us: "Sohail never gets angry about anything bad that happens to him; but he gets furious at injustice or harm done to someone else or some other group. Then, watch out, as he is merciless in his defence of that person or group."

I find that Sohail has mellowed over the years. His first personalized license plate said LOVING, the second said DARVESH, and the present one says HUMANIST. I think those plates symbolize the metamorphosis of Sohail starting from romantic flirt, progressing through a phase of focus on his guru self, to the mellower philosopher we know today.

This brings me to the book we are celebrating, *Love Letters to Humanity*. Sohail notes in his introduction that his main identity is as a writer, and that when he picks up his pen or, I suppose, sits down at his computer, he is most connected to his honest and intimate self. I suppose I have read just about everything he has written in English, and many of his works translated from Urdu, and looking back over the years and the writing, I would say that he has never written anything other than love letters to humanity. Whatever he has explored and discussed, from the psychology of suicide bombers to religious intolerance, to family violence to interpersonal conflict or social inequality and intolerance, he has never done what I call a dispassionate and intellectual review of the factors involved. Everything he writes carries a heartfelt plea, however subtle, for human beings to respect and care for one another as members of the same family. Whether letter, poem, essay, or short story, from the first work he ever created back in Pakistan, of which I have seen English translations, up to the book we are celebrating today, everything he has ever written has been, in one form or another, a love letter to humanity.

I join with everyone here in congratulating you, Sohail, on the publication of this beautiful book, and as one member of the human family of the world, I thank you for these love letters to me.

39. TWO THOUGHT PROVOKING BOOKS IN ONE
by Syed Haider

The title of the book, 'Words, Words And Words', and the blackness of the cover picture, first gave me the impression of a coal mine of words but far from it, as I burrowed through this mine it turned out to be a gold mine not of words but of thoughts, thoughts and thoughts. I found glittering nuggets of poems, colourful gems of short stories and sterling silver essays. Not surprisingly, among these beauties I found few dynamite sticks of thought which, in skillful hands, can be used to uncover new seams of deeper understanding. Articles on male dominance, secular spirituality, and the role of Urdu in promoting illiteracy in Pakistan are such smouldering explosives.

'Words, Words And Words' is one book but essentially there are two different books in one cover. Its short chapters and multiple perspectives pull the reader in immediately, and refuse to let him go. It is a well-written, well-structured and well-crafted book.

Take the chapter on poetry where both authors are musing on life, in all its apparent confusion as well as its simplicity and fleeting beauty. Many of the poems progress in unpredictable and tangential leaps, highlighting the consequences of combining the illusive Eastern search for wisdom with materialistic Western exuberance in the process. Dr. Sohail's Social Butterfly provides a good example:

I was a social butterfly
I used to go to parties and flirt
Flirt with
Young women, old women
Single women, married women
White women, black women

But gradually I lost interest in romance
And was enticed by wisdom
And that made her (his sweet heart)
Frustrated and angry and resentful
She left one night
And now
She goes to parties and flirts

Dr. K Sohail

Flirt with
Young men, old men
Single men, married men
White men, black men
She flirts with them all
She has become a social butterfly

The beauty of the poems in this collection is in communicating thoughts without using elaborate metaphors, abstract symbols and complex similes.

The two poems, A Darvesh Is Born and Social Butterfly are about transformation and change, as is the poem Wind My Companion. In the poem titled A Very Special Connection, the poets belief in a humanist ideology permeates every line, especially the concluding stanza:

"A sacred connection
A human connection
One day we will realize
We are all
Part of the same family
The human family."

The same theme of connection is found in the poem Sharing Dreams With You, but in a very romantic style.

The theme of Dr. Sohail's poem Unfinished Novel reminded me of Omar Khayyam's famous rubai in romantic style

"Ah, Love! could thou and I with Fate conspire
 To grasp this sorry Scheme of Things entire!
 Would not we shatter it to bits - and then
 Re-mould it nearer to the Heart's Desire!"

Dr. Khalid, in a preaching tone says:
"Time has come
For you to choose
Between
Your heavenly father
Who pushed you to violence and war
And
Your mother earth
Who is calling you
To a life of love and harmony and peace"

But at the end of poem poet admits:
"The irony is
We cant rehearse our roles
Or rewrite our scripts"

The last line, "Or rewrite our scripts", reminds me of the same dilemma faced by Omar when he said,
"The Moving Finger writes; and, having writ,
Moves on: nor all thy Piety nor Wit
Shall lure it back to cancel half a Line,
Nor all thy Tears wash out a Word of it."

Coincidently Dr. Sohail's collection of poems in this book ends on a short poem, Words, while Sain Sucha's collection starts with Wordist
His 'wordist' creates,
"From the soft and warm words
He shaped lullabies and chants
From Mellow, pretty and fragrant words
He created sonnets
With happy, joyful and glowing words
Waltzing, jumping and dancing words
He fashioned hymns and ballads."

In the next poem Sain Sucha wonders, what is truth?
"Is it
A rosary of shining edicts
Each perfectly cut and shaped
Sometime reveals to the elect
At times bestowed upon the so-called son
Or truth is
Occasionally claimed by some self-proclaimed messenger"

At the end of this poem Sain concludes his observation about truth by declaring:
"But However, you look at it
Truth can not be personal possession
Of any alleged heavenly or earthly being!
It is the collective pursuit and compilation of
Human knowledge
Its findings
Open to all for inquiry and authentication

Dr. K Sohail

Its fruits
Available to all for storage and utilization."

But is this available collective pursuit and compilation of human knowledge utilized properly by all? Not really, as appears in the poem, In The Hall of Mirrors,
"Every child is born innocent
With a clean sheath in the head
There is no feeling of hate and fear"

Then poet points out that,

"It is after the birth
The indoctrination starts
Adults feeding their own ideas of
Love and hate"

He concludes the poem by reminding us,
"In the hall of mirrors
Children are our own reflections"

Interestingly, in another poem, God In My House, the tables turn and the followers take charge.
"Eventually
The strings that make them move are
Left to be manipulated
By the hands of cunning disciples"

Sain Sucha forces the reader to confront questions of mortality, vulnerability and dependence in ways that are entirely his exclusively. His poems on truth, hope, ecstasy, elegy and loneliness are gold nuggets in this mine of thoughts, thoughts and thoughts.
It is neither easy nor recommended to compare the writing of the two authors but their shared antipathy towards traditional religion is plain. Even Buddha, whom progressives generally leave alone, is not spared. Sain Sucha is more blunt when he describes devoted disciples of God's self-proclaimed messengers.
"Each blinded by its glitter
Considering his set of commandments

To be the only set
His way to be the only way
Or
His book as the only book"

He enquires from Gautam Buddha—'Buddha ji'—about
the wellbeing of Moses, Jesus, Lord Kirshna and Prophet
Mohammad in a taunting way,
"And how about your other renowned friends
Among them
The chosen one
The only son
The one who plays on the flute
And
The receiver of final book"

Dr. Sohail's approach, on the other hand, is subdued
when he cautions all of the seven billion souls against divinity,
"You need to realize
Heavenly father is a fantasy
Mother earth is a reality
And you have to choose
Before it's too late"
The same alternating style of lukewarm and hot
continues in the prose, so instead of reviewing both authors
separately I will limit myself to the hotter one.

The seven short stories of Sain Sucha, explore subjects like
exploitation, war, destruction, remorse, social adjustment,
compromise, desire etc.
The first two expose the horrors of war: destruction by
missiles, artillery, bombs loss of innocent lives. Narrated in stark
and evocative prose, they use a weapons researcher and a war
photographer to brilliantly expose that we can not enlist half-
truths and false perceptions for long to prop up the master
drama of our own lives.
In Sixth Sense, we meet an ex-soldier who is turned into
a killing machine just six months after he was drafted into the
army. Trained to just kill mindlessly, after the war, he strives to
rid himself from the filth poured into his mind by military life. Just

as he begins to feel he has a handle on his passions and inner demons, an abrupt shift in perspective throws him into turmoil and he kills an innocent civilian.

The other four stories deal with social issues. In stories, Evil Eye and Rainbow, South Asian background and a young girl are the only two common factors in stories that deal with totally different subject matter.

Evil Eyes, depicts an interesting compromise between South Asian and Western outlooks:

""...I am Farakh sahib's middle daughter."

I knew Farakh had three daughters. But Farakh was a strict Muslim! ...

"I was thinking that Farakh sahib strictly believes in purdah. How come he allowed you to swim?"

She giggled again, "Daddy is not only open minded by his name but also in his thinking."...

"Then you observe purdah only from your father's friend?"

"Of course, only when daddy's friend from his old country visit us that we hide ourselves. After all, every one ought to protect oneself from evil eyes!""

Rainbow and Wet are about the intensity of sexual desire and getting satisfaction. Perhaps that is the reason that these two stories are written in abstract style. Writing such stories is a high-wire act of literary derring-do. The orderly grace of narrating the story may seem paradoxical when the author describes such intense, chaotic emotions. While the reader may at times feel bewildered, the sense of place and insight into the mysterious inclinations of the heart linger long after the last page.

These seven selected short stories continually undercut, enlarge and reshape our understanding of the enigmatic Sain Sucha, encircling his narrative with a type of sustained hard-boiled liberal thinking. But the more in-depth we go the more elusive he becomes.

At this point I will give very brief description of a few selected short stories by Dr. Sohail and move on to the essay section of the book

The first, A short Distance In A Long Time, deals with peaceful co- existence. The Message of this story is that all creatures should live peacefully and in harmony. It is a simple message but the clarity, compassion and understated anguish in the narrative gives this story a luminous grace.

Deep Love

Roots - Branches - Fruits, describes the perils and rewards of immigration in the lives of three brothers Mohammad, Khalid and Sohail; Mohammad the God fearing, Khalid the playboy and Sohail the in-between tackle the alien environment in their own ways.

The story, Bigamy, deals with conflicts arising when different cultures meet and their divergent traditions clash. Some victims find innovative solutions, like a woman marrying more than one husband, to resolve it and some fall apart for the lack of compromise.

Both Dignified Death Clinic and Island illustrate the effect of acute loneliness and the ultimate price those who suffer it choose to pay, while the moral of the story Devta, is that the seeds of happiness and prosperity are within us all.

All of above stories are presented in a reserved manner that allows for subtle moral and psychological shadings. On top of it Dr. Sohail is such a proficient storyteller that once you get started on one of his stories it is nearly impossible to let it go of.

The essay section contains five articles from Dr. Sohail on subjects like Human Psyche, Mystic Poetry, Story Telling, Evolution etc. They are great pieces of writing, refreshing, edgy, seductive, crisp, scholarly and illuminating hidden pockets of human heart. But if, along with the aforementioned characteristics, you are also interested in sizzling and unsettling articles you will find them in Sian Sucha's section of Essays.

Why illiteracy continues to prevail in Pakistan is one such article. Although it is a nine-page article we get first whiff of the subject matter on page 6 when the author finally turns his attention towards Pakistan. For another key word Illiteracy, you have to wait a little longer. Here is how Pakistan comes into the picture for the first time on page 6.

"In hotter Lahore the wind from the rose garden would overwhelm our visitor with arousing aromatic scent while burning sun rays bounce from the open petals and dazzle the eyes with glaring colours. The experience is exciting and orgasmic. "

The preceding 5 pages out of 9 contain scholarly and illuminating discussion on the origin and nature of speech and language starting from the very dawn of civilisation. The opening paragraph of this article sets the tone,

"Ever since human beings have accepted the nearness of each

other for social existence they have needed some sort of language for mutual communication."

From this opening, he goes on to describe the anatomy of language spoken as well as written. He identifies different writing methods like non-phonological and phonological systems and their branches and a lot of technical material. Thus, this article provides a vast and officious sweep of development of languages which makes this lengthy introduction worth reading.

The real thrust of the argument about why illiteracy continues to prevail in Pakistan is tackled on the last two pages. Here are a few interesting one-liners,

"In Pakistan the authorities, by insisting upon the people to learn to read and write Urdu, English or Arabic, have burdened the minds of their people...Had the authorities tried to teach these people to read and write their own languages the situation would definitely be a different one!...

Therefore, if the people of Pakistan want to raise their literacy then they must start with learning their own native language before any other."

And then the bomb shell,

"Quite preferably the languages of other provinces should be introduced in the primary schools of each province to facilitate intercommunication."

After reading Why Illiteracy Prevails In Pakistan, in which Urdu was identified as one of the suspects, I felt very uneasy when I started reading the other article on a similar topic, titled Urdu - Its Survival And Constancy. Sain Sucha is not a biased person but his harsh neutrality is evident when he uses terms like 'custodians of Urdu', 'defenders of Urdu for those poor souls who are guilty of speaking Urdu for reasons beyond their control. I myself am a guilty party too, because my parents, when they needed some sort of language for mutual communication, unfortunately choose poor Urdu. But as the article progressed, it put me at ease, especially the concluding paragraph assuring the reader that the author does not believe there is any danger of Urdu's demise as it is one of the major languages In today's world.

Even after this reassurance I got a few jolts here and there. For example, when we look at the material written in Urdu there is no shortage of so-called elitist literature. It abounds with poetry and prose of a high standard, but there is almost nothing in the non-fiction field. Initially I disputed this statement because I learned from Wikipedia that Urdu holds the largest collection of works on Islamic literature, but then I found plenty of circumstantial evidence in Sain Sucha's writing leading me to suspect he might be placing religion in the category of fiction. If that is the case then he is right, if you remove Islam Urdu has almost nothing in the non-fiction field.

Physical Laws, Human Beliefs And Natural disasters is another sharp piece of writing as many still believe physical laws are established by God for our benefit, the frequency and intensity of earthquakes, hurricanes and other natural disasters are actually optimized for our good. Sain Sucha, in his very short essay totally disagrees with that. His simple answer is that if you live by a volcano expect earthquake, flood if you live by river, landslides by mountain. The only way to avoid is to study the factors that cause them and to find a practical solution to control them. Furthermore, he questions why a God would first hit the people with a calamity and then come to help them? Although this is not a new controversy the author's position on this issue clearly reveals, in an unapologetic way, his atheistic approach and firm belief in science.

The article Male Dominance is an interesting composition of thoughts and opinions expressed by the author himself, as well as many other writers, on this subject. In this masterly and richly researched writing we may get lost sometimes but Sain Sucha's grip on the subject maintains enough control to keep us from wondering too far afield. After conducting in-depth analysis, the author identifies three reasons for male dominance. Their physical superiority and corresponding view of women as inferior, their obsession to control everything, and third, the lack of struggle from women to break the social chain. The article ends with this brilliant thought that every human being who is totally dependent upon the decision of another person for his own development is a subjugated person. This thought sounds like a good motto for women's struggle for equality.

In the end I thank Dr. Sohail and the Family of The Heart for giving me the opportunity to review this wonderful collection of prose and poetry.

Dr. K Sohail

40.   WORDS, WORDS AND WORDS
by Ishtiaq Ahmed

Words, Words and Words
by Dr. Khalid Sohail and Sain Sucha,
Joint Production of
Sollentuna, Sweden: Vudya Kitaban Förlag
Toronto, Canada: Green Zone Publishing, 2017
ISBN: 978-91-86620-42-4

Dr Khalid Sohail and Sain Sucha are two noted names on the global Pakistani literary landscape. They combine three quite distinct roles in their engagement with the public. They are poets, short-story writers and keen debaters of contemporary issues. Both have published books in Urdu and English and in the case of Sain Sucha also in Swedish. Both are natural scientists who have ventured into the spheres of sociology and philosophy. Dr Khalid Sohail is a practising psychiatrist while Sain Sucha runs a small publishing firm. Dr Sohail's parents moved from Amritsar to Lahore in 1947 while Sain Sucha hails from Mozang, Lahore. Like thousands of other educated Pakistanis, they moved to the West - Sohail to Canada and Sain Sucha to the UK and later Sweden.

'Words, Words and Words' is their joint English-language collaboration. The book is divided into three sections: the first covers poetry; the second short-stories; and the third contains their essays. The very title of the book is indicative of the significance and power they associate with words. Indeed, as far as we know, it is only human beings who have developed the skills to use words which become part of languages. Without words, there would be no history, no literature, no science, no philosophy. In fact, there would be no civilization.

From among Khalid Sohail's poems my eye fell on, Unfinished Novel. I quote some verses:

Each human being
Is an unfinished novel
That starts at birth
And is left unfinished at death......
The irony is
We can't rehearse our roles

Deep Love

Or re-write our scripts.
Sain Sucha won my heart with this poem: In the Hall of Mirrors
Every child is born innocent
With a clean sheath in the head
There is no feeling of hate or fear
For any
Caste, colour, race or religion
Only a natural love and affection
For the woman who gave the birth
No child is born evil!
It is after birth
That indoctrination starts
Adults feeding their own ideas of
Love and hate
Likes and dislikes
Pros and cons
Profits and losses

The short-stories the authors proffer capture some very interesting situations as one would expect from writers with their roots in two cultures—Pakistani/Canadian and Pakistani/Swedish—and their exposure to the global culture where seemingly incompatibles meet, clash but then peculiar combinations are formed.

Khalid Sohail's short-story, Bigamy, is a case in point. A Pakistani-Canadian Saif decides to go back to Pakistan because his brother has died suddenly and he feels duty-bound to help his family. That means marrying his sister-in-law. However, Saif is married to Susan in Canada. She feels betrayed and curses him. She decides to go to Pakistan and confront Saif. In the discussion which follows he explains that he married her also in a similar situation: she was married to an alcoholic and had small son to take care of. For a year she was seeing him secretly before she divorced her husband: so, in one sense she too lived in bigamy.

Susan began to understand Saif's predicament. She met Saif's uncle's first wife Razia, who could not bear children so the uncle married another woman without divorcing Razia, an arrangement she accepted because otherwise she would be without any support. For Susan, such situations began to make sense but what convinced her most to reconcile to bigamy was the story of Nooran, Razia's servant. Nooran was an extraordinarily beautiful woman when young. She belonged to a mountain-tribe in which brides were bought. She fetched Rs. 30,000 when the rate at that time was Rs. 10,000 for an average young woman. However, that was too big a sum. So, two men pooled Rs. 15,000 each and married her. She would spend one week with one husband and the next week with the other. Such customs were accepted by her tribe.

From among Sain Sucha's short-stories the one that left a deep impression on me is, Photo Finish. Peter, a Swedish photographer who specializes in covering armed conflicts began his career from Vietnam. Over the years he photographed other horrid wars such as the one in Cambodia, Bangladesh, Angola, Palestine, Iraq and Bosnia. Each such conflict had profoundly shocked him and yet he could not let go the itch to cover more.

This time it was Iraq again. Contemptuous of evil dictators who persecuted their own people as much as those who wanted to wage a war of destruction on Iraq in the name of peace, he reasoned he had to go because mounting bills needed to be paid.

The taxi arrives to fetch him to the airport. His little daughter Tindra comes running with swimming trunks while his wife Sandra looks on. Peter knows he is going to a place where there is no chance of swimming, although blood will be flowing in rivers. The journey towards the airport begins. Peter is suddenly reminded of the Vietnam war and that picture he took of a little girl running followed by her mother amid raining napalm bombs dropped by American aircraft. Seconds after that both were blown up.

Peter wonders what the mother and daughter were called: perhaps Sandra and Tindra. He imagines Sandra and Tindra running in front of him; Tindra holding his swimming trunks. He imagines going to the police station asking for them but the police can't help—he has no photograph of them. Suddenly he sees them again with a tank poised to come after them.

That scene jolts him back into the real world. He tells the taxi driver to drive back because he has left some important papers at home. At home, Sandra wonders what has happened. He tells her to give him the photo he took of her and Tindra last Mid-Summer Day. Sandra is surprised but Peter insists he wants to take their picture with him. The cruelty of war and the vulnerability of human beings are very ably portrayed by Sain Sucha in this short-story.

Both Khalid Sohail and Sain Sucha are known for taking bold, unconventional and non-conformist positions in their articles on contentious issues. I have selected Sohail's essay, Human Psyche... Soul or Mind, to present in this review. We all know that the human body is real and palpable but is there a soul which completes the body? The author points out that in the Judaeo-Christian and Islamic tradition a belief in the soul exists. In the Hindu-Buddhist tradition too the soul survives physical death. It returns in a cycle of reincarnations to purify itself until it is cleansed of all sin and temptation and joins the Supreme Spirit, God.

He then sets forth a model dealing with the physical and the mental in which the body and mind are one and do not exist as separate entities. This view has been advanced by Charles Darwin, Sigmund Freud, Karl Marx, Jean Paul Sartre and others. As a result, the importance of life is given far greater importance than what happens after death. Such an attitude has helped develop powerful arguments for making life on earth as fulfilling, safe and healthy as possible.

Sain Sucha's essay, Why Illiteracy Continues to Prevail in Pakistan, is a well-argued brief in favour of learning mother-tongues and several tongues simultaneously. He explains that besides the essential function of communication that all languages perform they also contain expressions, images and vocabulary which reflect the environment in which a language evolves, thus language reflects historical experience and culture. Consequently, people learn and express themselves best in a language in which they have been born and grown. He argues the reason illiteracy abounds in Pakistan is because instead of learning to read or write in their mother tongue, Punjabis are made to learn Urdu, English, Arabic and so on. He correctly points out that children can learn several languages and that should be encouraged, but not by ignoring those languages that supply the historical continuity in their social lives. Thus regional languages such as Punjabi, Sindhi, Pushto and Balochi should be the main language of instruction in school, while other languages can be taught simultaneously or in successive phases as the child grows up. With its examination of language theory, grammar and syntax, the essay is interesting for both specialists and the wider public alike.

Both authors are to be congratulated for writing their book – Words, Words and Words.

41. WORDS, WORDS, AND WORDS and THE SEEKER
by Aisha Isabel Ashraf

Good evening everyone. I'm very glad to be here with you today. I've had the good fortune to call Sohail my friend for a couple of years now. We're both immigrants who resist definition by culture, religion and social expectation, and as writers we have enjoyed many a discussion on the creative process and our experience of writing, so it was with great honour that I accepted his invitation.

The relationship between writer and reader is a complex one. The filter of personal experience means a reader's takeaway may not be what the author intended, and I hope I do justice to the crafting and care that Dr Sohail and Mr Sucha have brought to their work. If however I don't, I suppose we can look out for a particularly repugnant character by name of Aisha Ashraf in a future book.

While both of today's books emphasize a search for Truth, I'm starting with the collaborative work, "Words, Words, Words". In a society that pushes us to have an opinion on everything these are cautionary tales—reminders of the complexity of human nature in a world that likes things neatly explainable in an easy-to-remember sound bite, preferably with a link to share on Facebook or Twitter. In these days of misinformation and 'fake news' identifying truth grows more and more difficult but I came across the Forbes 2016 Index of Reputable Countries the other week, and with Sweden and Canada ranked #1 and #2 respectively we can surmise we're in good hands here.

When faced with the unwelcome prospect of emigration at the age of eight I responded by losing myself in books—I remember sitting on a kitchen chair engrossed in The Famous Five as things were wrapped, boxed, and carted off around me. Books are a natural refuge and there's a strong tradition of immigrants communicating their subjective truths on the page, whether to make sense of them for themselves or to share with others; we're never short of a tale to tell and this is undeniably migrant literature. I know labels are reductive but so is the 10 minutes I have to share these books with you so I've picked out what spoke loudest to me.

Sucha hooks the reader with humour, simplicity and alternate perspectives. He uses the imagery of everyday objects and events to open up heavy topics like theism, elitism, and truth to everyone. For example, In *'An Honest Request'* he speaks truth to power in the form of a letter to Buddha:

"Dear Buddha Ji:

How is it over there?

Are you still enjoying your Nirvana?"

He asks after the other 'renowned friends'…

"The chosen one

The only son

The one who plays on the flute

And

The receiver of the final Book"

before speculating on the five-star accommodation they're enjoying and enquiring if they ever look back and see the chaos they've left behind. He emphasizes the elitist nature of religious belief,

"You toiled for decades, and found what you looked for

And then you reached your Nirvana"

He makes us question the wisdom of basing a whole life on someone else's dream. What is the point of existence if we refuse to acknowledge our own as distinct from another's? If we smother our own individualism in order to copy?

Before this all gets too heavy he suggests a visit to straighten things out, but warns,

"Bring some divine protection with you on your way here

Lest you get executed by your own ardent disciples

Take advice from Jesus, he knows all about it!"

His sign-off is prosaic yet pointed,

"Looking forward to meeting you

And thanking you in anticipation

Your long abandoned friend

Sain Sucha"

In *'The God in My House'* he examines theism in the guise of a tactic all parents can relate to – the 'wait til your father gets home' threat.

"There is a god in my house

Called Pappa

He was not there

when I was alone

nor when I was married

Deep Love

But soon after
  my children were born
  He appeared
    first as a benign, helpful soul
      and then as a hard, punishing spirit
I have never known Him
Butmy wife and children
have lived with him for years"

Outlining the influence this deity has on their lives, he tells us,
"Pappa has functioned so successfully as a controlling
factor all the years my wife found Him convenient
He has been her best friend!
He was my wife's creation"

And just when we're smiling in recognition of a crafty parenting hack he tosses us this:
"And now I wonder
  if all GODS are created that way?"
  Sucha's poems start simply and expand to encompass the universal. He challenges us to see things differently, with an 'earthiness' that speaks to the reader as an equal. No one could accuse the author of *'In Praise Of Shit'* of being preachy. He's just reminding us of what he's confident we already know.
"Praise the shit
That removes all differences
And make us aware
We are all equal
In our hour of need."

  While sharing themes of Connection, Truth and Religion, Sohail writes of spiritual maturation, a realization of the interconnectedness of things. In *'Appreciating What You Are Not'* he claims,
"What you are not
Is as significant as what you are"
pointing out the need for contrast to see things as they really are. In art the areas around and between objects in a painting are called 'negative space' and they influence how we perceive the piece as a whole—Sohail applies this idea to the contradictions and contrasts within a person, invisible to the self

until *'you can see them in my smiling eyes.'* His tone of calm, nurturing peace runs throughout the poems in numerous affectionate addresses, 'my children', 'my love', 'my friend'.

The journey of learning to see and work with what you have—recognition and acceptance—is skilfully portrayed in *'Wind, My Companion'*. Citing the misery and injustice he saw when last they walked together the narrator declines the Wind's invitation to explore. But Wind responds,

"One journey and you go whimpering,
dejected and depressed.
Look at me
Do you see me surrendering to the realities of life?"
He stresses the importance of hope,

"...wherever I go,
I sing a melody of joy,
For you must know that the quitters will be trampled upon
while the song lives on."

The narrator realizes that strength lies in connection to one another, in spite of difference or hardship, a connection created by something as simple as a smile, a song, kindness, or encouragement. By the end of the poem he's ready to continue his learning journey. Recognizing the limits of his understanding he turns his face again towards growth,

"My strength returned,
My wounds began to heal.
I did not understand the whole truth
But I wanted to learn more."

Both writers' poems expand to hold a wider meaning. In each there is an 'opening out' from one person to another, from one view to another, from the subjective to the holistic.

These themes continue in the stories. We meet characters facing change and difference, we watch to see if they stiffen and dig in, or open themselves to the uncertainty of not having all the answers. Both writers use different points of view and gender to press their questions, searching for ways to reach beyond our existing beliefs and show us something that was there all along.

Sucha's characters are largely unpleasant—lascivious, angry, resentful and sullen—which is great news for us because he's at his best when writing thoroughly disagreeable people into existence. Through his careful layering of personality we come to an appreciation of their viewpoint, even if we don't share it. We can recognize their vulnerabilities and shortcomings and it becomes difficult to dislike them outright.

Sohail's characters speak to a broader experience, a willingness to look outwards—an openness that is absent in Sucha's protagonists who can no longer see things as they really are. Claustrophobic and dark, his characters are rats trapped in a maze, unaware of their imprisonment.

Both authors speak of opposing ideas existing simultaneously and the need to accept and work with this. Sucha's narrator in *'The Evil Eyes'* pauses to reflect,

"It was a strange day – I had gained my peace of mind by two different and opposite ways!"

In *'Roots – Branches – Fruits'* Sohail's narrator overhears this exchange,

"The children of immigrants are very unusual... either they become artists or they lose their minds."

"Why?"

"Because they have to carry the burden of their traditions while facing the challenge of their environments. If they succeed they become artists... otherwise they become insane."

There's a preoccupation with duality and the grey areas between polarities. We are reminded of the many faces of good and evil, and how even god has no single face.

For Sohail, the character is a fulcrum for pivoting perspective; for Sucha's characters that perspective is often attained too late.

The essays both writers include underline what drives them. Sucha is concerned with communication in a concrete, pragmatic sense—gender imbalance, illiteracy in Pakistan, how blind belief influences behaviour. Sohail is more abstract, walking us along the line between the spiritual and the functional, the point where the storyteller and the psychiatrist meet. He writes about mystic poetry and storytelling. Why do we tell stories? To teach, to connect, to explore, to be free. At the same time he traces the development of medicine beyond the traditional religious approach, sharing how a neurologist's stroke revealed a biological basis for higher consciousness that exists in us all, not just mystics.

The three arenas of Poetry, Story and Essay encourage

us to draw links between things where before we might only have seen distinctions and in this, at the very least, the authors have achieved their ambition.

In his 'short, very short, auto-biography', *'The Seeker'*, Sohail has managed to capture the personal while sidestepping the spotlight with his subtitle: *The Story Of Khizr And His Search For Truth*. Khizr literally means 'The Green One', with green symbolizing the freshness of knowledge drawn from the living sources of life and it links nicely with the Greenzone philosophy he founded that underpins his work as a psychotherapist. Life is the central theme here, finding a way to see it for what it truly is, without squinting through the lenses of another man's glasses. The first chapter opens with,
"Only a few people are fortunate enough to discover in their lifetime that life can be so mysterious, mystical and magical. And Khizr was one of them."
In Muslim tradition, Khizr is the spiritual guide of Moses and hidden initiator of those who walk the mystical path. Who better to embody Sohail in his search for Truth?
Memoir is an increasingly popular way to discuss the lessons learned over the course of a life. In one way it's a creative nonfiction narrative, in another it includes certain fictional elements in the way the story is constructed so that readers from all walks of life can relate to it. Before a book can be written, one of the most important decisions a writer must make concerns the type of memoir they wish to offer readers. Instead of structuring his story in a traditional format Sohail gave it a unique twist, personalizing the concepts and ideas he wanted to cover through the people who made an impact on him in the course of his life, thus, his mother was Religion, his father Mysticism, and his uncle Creativity. Pakistan became The Land of Tradition, and Canada The Land Of Freedom. Even the title of 'Contents' above the list of chapters is replaced by the infinitely more personal 'Encounters'.
We all know humans are complicated, and the beauty of this book, I think, is its simplicity. The story becomes a stand-in for our own experiences, encouraging us to examine our involvement with these same concepts. I read this in one go and halfway through I knew it was something I would read again. Albert Einstein said, "The definition of genius is taking the

complex and making it simple." The concepts Sohail presents in these bite-size chapters are weighty subjects covering influential ideas from the arts and sciences, but he distils them into something graspable and still manages to weave in a sense of fable and timelessness that transcends one person's life.

In *'The Seeker'* Sohail, you have successfully united all the different 'selves' that gave us your previous books. Khizr carries the scientist, the therapist, the humanist, and the poet simultaneously within, and this 'short, very short auto-biography' is a fitting, beautifully written summation of 65 years of discovery and learning.

Happy Birthday!

Dr. K Sohail

42. *IN QUEST OF... THE SEEKER*
by Christen Junker-Andersen

Ladies and gentlemen:

First and foremost, I wish to convey my sincerest congratulations and heart-felt best wishes to my friend, Dr. Khalid Sohail, both on attaining his 65th birthday and on the publication of his latest book, "The Seeker". In Sohail's "Land of Tradition", and in many other parts of the world today, to successfully reach the age of 65, and to do so while holding and championing personal beliefs and opinions that run contrary to the established mainstream, is an achievement that is often attended by a certain amount of good luck and no small measure of personal risk. Congratulations, Sohail. That such a situation definitely does not prevail here in Canada, Sohail's "Land of Freedom", is a gift that our recent national sesquicentennial has, I hope, allowed us all to reflect upon with gratitude.

Secondly, I wish to express my thanks to you all for allowing me to be here today. I very much look forward to becoming acquainted with as many of you as possible as I have long wished to meet the members of Dr Sohail's extended Family of the Heart. I have heard a great deal about many of you and your individual accomplishments, and I must confess to being rather intimidated by the collective breadth of experience and the wealth of knowledge and talent that you, the audience, encompass.

I was also somewhat nonplussed by the idea of delivering an oral book review before a "live" audience; something I don't think I've done since Grade 6, an experience that for me was more than a little traumatic and one which I did not and do not care to repeat. Nevertheless, I acceded to Sohail's request to address you this evening out of my considerable respect for him and his continuing work, and to honour the apparent esteem that he in turn accords my own opinions. (I fail to understand why the latter should be the case but, what the heck, I'll go with it ... .)

It is normally the task of a serious reviewer to summarize, analyse and critically evaluate the text under examination. Still, I don't feel that it is altogether either necessary or appropriate to offer you a simple assessment, appraisal, or critique of "The Seeker"; which has already been thoroughly reviewed by several others, even within its own covers. In all honesty, I don't think there's an awful lot I can say that hasn't already been said. I hope, therefore, that you will bear with me, as I may wander perhaps a little bit further afield. Nevertheless, I shall do my duty, as assigned.

In his new book, "The Seeker", subtitled "The Story of Khizr and His Search for Truth", Dr Sohail presents the essential kernels of his autobiography in the form of a series of allegorical parables and aphorisms that focus on the character of "Khizr", his journey from his youth in the "Land of Tradition" to his maturity in the "Land of Freedom", and his interactions with the actors in the play who influence him most strongly throughout his life. These important individuals are each referred to by the single trait that best describes their character and personality. Thus, Khizr's mother is Religion, his father Mysticism, his grandmother Wisdom, his sister Friendship, his teacher Science, and so on. And from each, Khizr draws an important lesson that helps him move ever further along the highway of life. But through it all, Khizr's journey is marked by his quest for veritable truth, understanding, and wisdom, accompanied by his sincere desire to help others find the path to their own personal epiphanies, enlightenment and creative expression.

Sohail's unique choice of this allegorical form at once allows him to tell his own story in such a way that the details of Khizr's life are readily recognizable as Sohail's own by those who know him, while also serving to highlight the important events of Khizr's/Sohail's life in a manner that lends the weight of universal experiential truth. For many of his readers, Khizr's history will often reflect and relate to their own lives in ways that may seem eerily familiar.

In my own case, for example, I grew up as a "child of the 60s", an idealistic refugee from the "summer of love". I also longed for a world in which "peace and good, [and] brotherhood" (apologies to Tommy James, et al.), love, open minds, and non-judgmental acceptance and even the celebration of peoples' differences would be the governing factors in both interpersonal and international relations.

My personal pursuit of such altruistic goals was characterised by several years of social and political activism that were largely ended by such discouragements as the shootings at Kent State University in 1970 and the ruthless suppression by "Metro's Finest" of the protests that followed that event five days later at the US Embassy in Toronto and participation in numerous similar events over the ensuing years. For me, this part of my life was accompanied by a period of spiritual and religious exploration and experimentation, which ultimately ended in disappointment, disillusionment, disgust, and depression.

Like Sohail's Khizr, I came to deplore religion, superstition and hypocrisy in all their forms, and to distrust and even despise the priests and politicians who habitually delude their followers with self-serving promises and lies and fill their heads with impossible dreams and hatred. But I also came to appreciate and value humanity, compassion, the pursuit of knowledge through the sciences and free and unfettered discourse, the power of rational, critical thought, and finally the wisdom to know when to speak and when to shut up. (I still have a hard time with that last one, just ask my wife!)

I am telling you all this by way of explaining that, for me, many of the events and experiences, and even several of the characters encountered in Khizr's life, as related by Sohail, are almost indistinguishable from my own. But where I was defeated by life's vicissitudes, Khizr/Sohail, made of sterner stuff, gained wisdom from them. He rose above the mundanities and exigencies of the daily struggle for existence and ultimately earned international recognition as a humanist, writer, poet, and innovative therapist. In short, in every field to which he has turned his hand, he has achieved notable success. His words, therefore, are not to be taken lightly.

Sohail's choice of the character named Khizr as his avatar is an interesting one. Early in his life, Khizr reports on his ongoing crisis of faith and quest for veritable truth. In that context, the use of the name Khizr is appropriate insofar as, in English, that name may be translated to mean "Seeker". On the other hand, Khizr (or Khidr or al-Khidr, et al.) is a figure described in the Quran as a trusted and righteous "Servant of God", possessing great wisdom or mystic knowledge, a messenger, prophet, or guide. According to Wikipedia, he has been identified in other traditions as Vishnu, Sorūsh, Sarkis the Warrior, and even St. George and John the Baptist within various Christian traditions. For a man who has achieved significant recognition as an avowed atheist and secular humanist, there is not a little irony in his choice of alter ego. Are we to infer, then, that Khizr, and by extension Sohail himself, has achieved some form of nirvana? In the book, Khizr, the seeker, ultimately becomes Khizr, the guide; the student is become the teacher, the Darvesh. Is Sohail showing us a path to emotional, intellectual and spiritual truth and enlightenment that is without recourse to religion or belief in a god or gods?

Sadly, the closing pages of the book seem to presage the closing of Khizr's life. Old and tiring of his life's quest for truth and wisdom, he determines to pass the torch, as it were, to his children and grandchildren. To us.

This is the gift of love that Sohail offers his readers: a deceptively simple, at times even lyrical story of a man's life and quest that can be read, understood, and appreciated on several meaningful and even deeply personal levels. In this small book, reminiscent as it is in many ways of the writings of Kahlil Gibran and Hermann Hesse, Sohail provides us with enough astute observations and trenchant aphorisms to warrant its repeated reading; something I think that I shall be doing repeatedly in the years to come.

Thank you Sohail.
And thank you all for your attention.

Christen Junker-Andersen, M.A.
July 9, 2017

43.   DR. KHALID SOHAIL'S 'DEEP LOVE'
by Zahir Anwar

A few years ago, Dr. Khalid Sohail sent me one of his books titled, *Love Letters to Humanity.* The book made interesting reading and dealt, at length, with his thoughts and dreams of a better world. He expressed himself elegantly as a humanist and a psychotherapist. The book is a collection of his poems, essays and translations. The reader could appreciate the author's dreams. The book was 'dedicated to the dreams of a just and peaceful world'. But the blurb on the last page, by the inimitable master story teller, Joginder Paul, declares in no uncertain terms that he was 'moved' by his capacity of love. He wrote, " *After all these years of involvement in creative writing, I have come to believe firmly that the relevance and survival of literature and the literary artist depends primarily on his capacity of love and to suffer in fellowship, not on, as some writers appear to believe, a patchwork of clever and callous writing done in self-celebration."*

In the above lines one finds the quintessence of the present book titled, *Deep Love,* by Dr. Khalid Sohail, a writer, psychotherapist, poet, an essayist, and last but not the least, a humanist. The book contains a collection of biographical, creative and professional essays and his philosophical conclusions that embrace not only his desire for a better and a secular world but also express the gradual evolution of the human race. As regards his style, he prefers a very simple and lucid way of expression that is always intelligible to his readers. He appears knowledgeable and wise. Temporary superficial fame has never been his target. He seems to address the intellectuals as well as the masses in general in his new book focusing on love and creativity, human evolution and the dream of a secular society.

Anne Henderson aptly opines about him, *"He never stops thinking, creating and writing."* Dr. Sohail's curiosity about anything and everything keeps his dynamic creative urge in constant motion. He can create at any given opportunity and write a poem on any beautiful sight. I have seen him making the most of his 'creative lunch breaks' which he has used to benefit his creative writing. This book seems a creative continuation of his previous books including *From Islam to Secular Humanism* and *Prophets of Violence, Prophets of Peace.* In his book *The Next Stage of Human Evolution* he discusses human psychology, science and humanism and nurtures hope for a world full of peace and harmony, instead of unwanted death and destruction brought about by the fanatical religious bigots in the world. He is of the opinion that the choices human beings make individually and collectively must be positive by evolving in the right direction and caring for one another's needs, gracefully and generously to transform the dream of a peaceful world into reality.

Here, in this book, Dr. Sohail is in eternal quest for peace and love, pursuing his relentless process of finding solutions for human problems and social justice. A practicing psychotherapist, his prolific writings have reached fruition in most of his creative endeavours—Urdu and English, poem and prose. Perhaps he has, like Alberto Moravia, one great tune to play and that is love for humanity. He is indeed one of the most secular human beings I have ever come across. He deals with his topics with a strange kind of intellectual freedom and expresses them with imagination. He writes in a simple way what he feels inside his sanctum, sanctorum---his mind and heart.

The book encompasses his vast reading, including his assessment of Dr. Jill Taylor's book *My Stroke of Insight* which inspired him. *Deep Love* brings together his accumulation of knowledge acquired through various books and his personal experiences over a long period of time and uncovers for us a different world which is so intimate and urgent, so close to our time and yet lingers vividly in the past. By going through his book and his vast contributions, I can safely vouch that 'there will always be singing in the dark times' and more so when Dr Sohail is in sublime and inspirational mood or in a sort of heavenly and divine mental exhilaration. The readers will never find any kind of 'patchwork of clever and callous writing done in self-celebration.' We also hear the echoes of a number of great minds all through the book in support of his thesis. In almost all of his books, he has taken care to move forward and tread carefully, never ever stepping over the philosophies and theories of the great philosophers and scientists who have guided him to arrive to his conclusions.

I would like to add a few words on the use of his

language. The Indian and Pakistani writers writing in English date back to the year 1800 and as a vehicle of communication, a great many writers, despite their love-hate relationship to colonialism, developed their unique style, almost at equal footing with the native English writers. What makes Dr. Sohail's writing more alluring and humane is the warmth, feeling and excitement with which he infuses his language and ideas. There is also a kind of austerity in his style which readers can hardly miss. This is the way he explores profound truth and incites his readers to arrive at the relationship with his message of love, beauty and creativity. Thus, his contributions become all the more significant in our troubled times. The style of his writing is unique and exemplary, almost at par with other creative Anglo-English writers of his age. Readers can see for themselves in his leisurely winding narratives:

"Artists redefine our concept of good based on aesthetic rather than moral values. Artists help us to appreciate the beauty of nature and humanity and get in touch with our inner beauty. They help us to develop our Right Brains in order to appreciate words, colours, sounds and in doing do, touch the artist inside all of us. They help us keep alive our inner child to play and enjoy life."

He speaks directly, in a language which is at once simple, humane and easy to comprehend the lesson inherent therein for the solidarity of the human race. This is vintage Khalid Sohail, always in a state of approval of positive construct in our cultural perspectives, his structural base to express both the beauty and ugliness of life. He is a humanist who is also a feminist (many of his poems can be cited) and a psychotherapist.

In all of his writings he seems to echo the prophetic utterance of Albert Camus that the purpose of a writer is to keep civilization from destroying itself. He constantly seeks knowledge from the great minds of the past and present and weaves in his narrative such materials to showcase the ever-changing history of human evolution. He inspires us to question traditions based on obsolete religious and cultural values at a time when the world has suffered so much on account of fanaticism, terrorism, insurgencies and highhandedness of state machineries. He outlines, from his study of great philosophers and scientists ' a secular discipline of human psychology' and advocates 'the humanist traditions in which our understanding of human mind and personality is based on our scientific and secular principles rather than Holy Scriptures." It now remains to be seen whether his path-breaking dreams can make deep inroads in the minds of readers. In our teens, being radical, we had dreams which remain unfulfilled till this day. We will pine for a society constructed on equality where peace and justice reign supreme and scientific enquiry and reason prevail over revelation and divinity. Nevertheless, no 'isms' or 'philosophy' political or otherwise, could bring about a change so drastic and we are still face-to-face with extreme fanaticism and global terror. The journey of human evolution, from its ancient traditional roots to a secular humanistic state, is still to be realized fully and most of us at present appear to be disillusioned. Dr. Sohail, however, is not a pessimist but a sort of romantic saint who keeps on dreaming of a better world based on secular and scientific credentials full of love and inner beauty. His philosophical essays are full of unforgettable insights about the mind, soul and evolutionary process of our changing society. He seems to conclude that 'blind faith' and organized religion are indeed things of the past and a secular world of love, peace, equality and fraternity lies in the hands of science, psychology and philosophy, and the future of the human race depends largely on social changes that took place 'over the centuries' and paid a 'heavy price for challenging old traditions'. Even as an individual and particularly in an era of dubious distinction when men are known for duping men and consumerism rules the roost, Dr Sohail creates a strong connection with the upcoming talents of his city as well as authors from other parts of the world, provides them with the creative platform of the *Family of the Heart* for expressing their thoughts and ideas so that the larger public become aware of the power of words, colours, sounds and various ideologies. Here, at the platform, they showcase their writings before a thinking audience and strengthen our bond in an amazing way, preserving our diverse cultural history through dialogue, debate and resolution. Here we can find a hint of a world without boundaries of nations. Never ever was the need so urgent than the present moment. *Deep Love* deserves all our attention as the content of the book is meant for a better, tolerant and more humane world based on science and reason. Dr. Sohail says clearly at one stage of the book:

Dr. K Sohail

"I am of the opinion that blind faith and religion were our past and science, psychology and philosophy are our future as human beings. On the journey of human evolution we are gradually evolving from religious communities and theocratic states to secular communities and humanistic states where all citizens will enjoy equal rights and privileges."

He expresses his thoughts so lucidly, urging us to focus on the immediate and larger issues of humanity. His deep concern slowly but steadily strives for international brotherhood and creates a bridge among different communities and cultures, helping us create a better understanding among all.

The book, in style and content, connects admirably with the author's earlier and equally important book *The Next Stage of Human Evolution,* drawing heavily upon his experiences as a psychotherapist and his philosophical approach to human evolution through his unique reference to men of letters. Here the discussions originated through his biographical essays and understanding of the minds of his conventional and mystical father and his illustrious atheist uncle that led him to the logical selection of 'the path of peace and harmony rather than violence and war." The author seems to have spent a lifetime pursuing the logical conclusions of his thoughts and experiences. He seeks to create a climate of change for a better world order and a secular environment at a time when our universe is dangerously threatened by fundamentalism and coercion and in this particular sphere, the book appears to be prophetic in dispelling the source of *fear* and lays the foundation of true mental freedom.

www.ingramcontent.com/pod-product-compliance
Lightning Source LLC
Chambersburg PA
CBHW051243250626
47155CB00009B/3147